GW00642639

DR SHEWELL-COOPER'S
BASIC BOOK OF
NATURAL GARDENING

BASIC BOOK OF NATURAL GARDENING

W. E. SHEWELL-COOPER
MBE, NDH, FLS, FRSL, Dip.Hort.(Wye), DLitt

BARRIE & JENKINS
COMMUNICA-EUROPA

© W. E. Shewell-Cooper 1978

First published in 1978
by Barrie and Jenkins Ltd
24 Highbury Crescent, London N5 1RX

All rights reserved. No part of this
publication may be reproduced in any
form or by any means without the prior
permission of Barrie & Jenkins Ltd.

ISBN 0 214 20421 9

Printed in Great Britain by litho at The Anchor Press Ltd
and bound by Wm Brendon & Son Ltd
both of Tiptree Essex

TO
MY WIFE
IRENE R. SHEWELL-COOPER

Contents

Acknowledgements

The author would like to thank the following for supplying black and white photographs and transparencies.

Robert J. Corbin 5; Harry Smith 6, 9, 15, 17, 22; Pat Thomas 16.

List of illustrations

Black and white photographs and line drawings

Preface

No gardening author can ever claim that the whole book is his own. He has learnt so much from others; so many have helped with advice, that a gardening book becomes the experience of a large number of people, welded together by one – in this case by one who has gardened for very many years.

Special thanks are due to Miss Gweneth D. Johnson, Dip. Hort. (Swanley), FGGA, former Technical Assistant at the International Advisory Bureau, who has corrected the proofs and taken care of the drawings. I should also like to thank the members of the Good Gardeners' Association at Arkley Manor, and my secretary, Mrs B. Lovelock, who typed all the script effectively.

W. E. SHEWELL-COOPER

Arkley Manor
Arkley
Herts.

1 Soil

Many people look upon soil as an inert mass, and rather a dirty inert mass at that. In fact soil is the place where roots can grow, to anchor the plants down. It is also a reservoir from which the roots can extract dissolved mineral substances. But the best way, perhaps, to regard soil is to think of it as a very large manufacturing centre where millions of living organisms (bacteria) are working all the time. Some of them will work to break down plant foods and turn them into a form that the root hairs can take in, while others, if given the chance, will try and build up these materials into a form that *cannot* be used by the plant, in order to conserve the foods for the time being.

Our main object in treating the soil (from the cultural point of view) should be to see that these bacteria are given the conditions they like, so that they can multiply and work in an unrestricted manner. If bacteria were not present, the soil would be sterile, and could not support plant growth at all. We must therefore encourage the soil bacteria by seeing that the soil (1) is well aerated, (2) is sufficiently moist, (3) contains enough lime, and (4) is warm enough. The organisms work at their best at about 65 degrees F, and cease to work above about 100 degrees F and below 10 degrees F.

THE ORIGIN OF SOIL

Soil is produced by agencies that have been at work for thousands of years disintegrating rocks. This 'weathering' is caused by heat and frost, by rain and running water, by the cracking and pounding of rocks by glaciers, and so on. In addition, the material so produced may have been carried down in turn to the plains by floods or by gravity, and so new types of rock have been produced. These rocks may, in their turn, have been pulverized, and so many varied types of soils are found all over the country. Because of the movement of soils, surface soil can seem quite unrelated to the earth down below. We must accept the soil as we find it in our gardens, and learn to treat it in the best manner possible.

TYPES OF SOIL AND HOW TO TREAT THEM

There are five main types of soil: clay, loam, sand, chalk (or lime) and peat. Of course, even these soils differ, and you can have combinations of one or more of them, such as clayey loams and sandy loams. And the soil itself can consist of one type and the subsoil of another. A soil testing kit, available from chemists and seed shops, will tell you what kind of soil you have.

SANDY SOILS

These consist of very small particles of silica and quartz. The amount of humus (see page 14) present in them alters the colour and the texture. A sandy soil is light and, of course, dry. It is one of the warmest soils and, because of its dryness, it warms up quickly in the spring. For this reason it is useful for producing early crops. One of the advantages of a sandy soil is that it can be worked at any time of the year and is easy to cultivate. On the other hand it is poor in plant foods, and does not retain moisture easily.

CLAY SOILS

These are putty-like, and smooth and silky to the touch. Even when well drained, this type of soil is wet, and difficult to cultivate during rainy periods and in the winter months. If it is dug when wet, it has the nasty habit of settling down – or 'panning' as it is called – like cement, when it is very difficult to work. Clays should be dug (if digging is done at all) in the autumn and left rough, so that the action of the frost and wind can pulverize them, and make them into an easily workable condition in the spring. These soils are said to be late, because it is impossible to get on them as early as sandy soils in the spring. The crops produced are later also.

On the other hand, clay soils are much richer in plant foods than sand, and this, in addition to their water-retention properties, makes them valuable in a dry season. It is important to see that clay soils are drained, and this is one of the best ways of improving them. Lime should be applied to clay soils as it prevents them from becoming so sticky and opens them up.

LOAM

The best way of describing a loamy soil is to say that it is an ideal blend of sand and clay. The sand keeps the soil open, and the clay ensures sufficient moisture-retention properties. There are various types of loams, depending on the proportion of clay or sand present. In old gardening books the word loam appears continuously as being the best soil for large numbers of plants. Of course the ideal loam has all the advantages of sandy and clay soils, and none of their disadvantages.

CALCAREOUS OR CHALKY SOILS

These are very deficient in plant food and rather shallow as a rule. They are lacking in humus, and as much organic matter as possible should be added every year. They are often chalky because they overlie chalk or limestone, and fine particles of these substances may be found every time the land is cultivated. When wet they are sticky, and so are difficult to work during rainy periods. In dry seasons they are disappointing, as they suffer from lack of water. The chalk can cause the leaves of plants to become bright yellow in colour, a condition known as chlorosis. This yellowing may not affect the plants in any other way, but it usually means stunted growth. Chalky soils seldom need lime, and the club root disease of cabbages does not usually flourish.

Into this group one ought perhaps to put what are known as the marls, though these are really a chalky clay. In the garden they are treated in the same way as clay soils, except that, again, dressings of lime are not necessary.

PEATY SOILS

The most outstanding feature of peaty soils is that they are absolutely devoid of lime, and so are very 'sour'. This sourness is produced by the decaying of the vegetable matter present. Such soils contain more than 20 per cent of humus. Peats have usually been derived from marshland where there has been continuous growth for thousands of years. They are often low-lying, and so may be waterlogged and may need pipe draining. Certain crops, like celery, do very well on peaty soils and what are known as moss lands in Lancashire and Cheshire are evidence of this. Brown peat is more easy to bring into cultivation than the black, heavy, bog-like peat. Once peaty soils are well worked and limed, they can prove valuable. Some plants, like rhododendrons and azaleas, prefer these soils to any other.

SOIL COLOUR

Soils differ in colour according to the amount of humus they contain, but moisture plays its part in giving a darker or lighter appearance also. Soils that are full of organic matter are dark and warm up quickly (that is one of the reasons why it is so important to add compost, ie properly-rotted organic matter, each year), while soils with little organic matter are light in colour. When there is a good deal of iron oxide present the soil will look red or yellow. The beautiful red soils of Devon are usually in a high state of fertility because a good deal of organic matter is present, together with iron oxide, and so these soils are generally sufficiently moist also. Soil colour matters in that it indicates the soil's 'contents'.

SUBSOILS

The best garden soils are about a foot in depth, but many gardens have soil no deeper than 8 or 9 ins. Below this top layer is the subsoil, which may be similar in character to the material above, and yet which will not contain millions of living bacteria or available plant foods. Subsoil affects the gardener, chiefly because it either allows or impedes drainage. For instance, if you have a light loam over gravel or sand all excess moisture will be quickly carried away. It is unfortunate, however, to have an easily workable loam over heavy clay, as the movement of water is impeded and the surface is apt to get waterlogged.

HUMUS

Humus is a brownish-black 'jam' or 'jelly' produced from the decaying vegetable matter in the soil, or any old manure or compost that has been purposely added, and of course from the leaves and roots of former plants. One of the reasons that well rotted and composted farmyard manure is so popular is that it not only adds plant food to the soil, but it increases the organic or humic content also.

Humus tends to act like a sponge and to hold moisture for the plant roots. In itself it produces plant foods, and the acids and gas given off during the process of rot help to free and preserve other plant foods that would otherwise be useless and not available to plants. Humus darkens soil and tends to warm it. It is vital to build up the humus content of a soil.

All sorts of chemical changes occur during the formation of humus, and the soil organisms work on the carbohydrates and proteins, breaking them down into simpler substances. Gases are formed in the soil during this process and these are the cause of more work. To be effective, humus must be continually replenished, and it will then maintain garden soils in a suitable physical condition.

The important thing to remember is that humus is not 'dead' – it is the transition stage between one form of life and another. Keep in mind that there is an organic cycle and that there are changes and processes constantly going on.

MULCHING

The movement of water in soil is both upward and downward. The excess water gradually percolates through, and, if the drainage is perfect, is carried away. Because of the porosity of soil the water may rise also, and when the water gets to the top of the soil the heat of the sun may evaporate it, and the wind carry it away. In this way soils can be dried out in hot weather. To prevent this evaporation of soil moisture, mulching is carried out. It can take two forms: (1) the continued cultivation of the top half-inch or inch of soil – known as dust mulching, or, much better still, (2) the application of organic matter – say compost or sedge peat. These methods have the effect of keeping the water where it is required, ie round the roots of the plants.

Mulching is usually carried out in early summer months for this purpose. Modern organic gardeners adopt the mulching method all over the garden. They apply the powdery dark brown compost to beds of roses, flowering plants, shrubs etc., 1 in. deep. Annual weeds then do not grow, and so there is no hoeing to be done. Where proper compost has not been made sedge peat is used instead at the same rate.

This top dressing is not renewed every year as some people think – it is left as a top dressing until it is pulled in by the worms. When it has been absorbed in the soil in this way a further top dressing is given.

In the vegetable garden put the powdery compost on the soil in, say, early November and let it lie. The worms will pull the bulk of the organic matter into the soil, and by the time spring comes it will only be necessary to rake the soil over as deeply as possible, and the earth will then be ready for seed sowing.

Under this system no actual digging is done at all.

DIGGING

BASTARD TRENCHING

Bastard trenching is perhaps the most commonly practised

digging operation. The very fact that the top spit of soil contains plant foods in an available form, and that the under spit has in all probability never been weathered, encourages gardeners to keep these at their normal levels.

Mark out on the piece of ground to be dug a strip 2 ft wide, and then remove the top spit and wheel it to the end of the plot where the digging will finish. Get into the trench thus made, and dig it up well, leaving the dug soil where it is; if the soil tends to be heavy, a fork is the best tool for this purpose. Place the compost on top of the forked ground, together with annual weeds and any other rotted material you may have. Then move the line back another 2 ft, and, spadeful by spadeful, cover in the first trench with the top soil from this area. In this way another trench, similar in size to the first one, is formed, which you should treat in the same way. Continue this operation until you reach the other end, where you will find the heap of soil to fill in the last trench made.

It is possible to divide the piece of ground to be dug into two portions (use a line), and then to dig down the whole of one strip round the end of the plot, and come up to the top of the other strip, where you will have placed the pile of soil from the first trench. If you want to increase the fertility of the lower soil you can not only place the compost on top of the dug-out bottom of the trench, but, when forking, actually fork compost into this as well.

SINGLE DIGGING
This consists of turning the ground over to one spade's depth, and is often done in the summer when the gardener is in a hurry to prepare for another crop. A shallow trench is always taken out to start with.

FORKING AND RAKING
Other operations normally carried out in the spring or summer are forking and raking, both of which are designed to get the soil into a fine condition suitable either for sowing seeds or putting out plants. This condition is known as a fine tilth. In the autumn leave the land rough, and in the spring and early summer prepare the fine tilth. The rake is designed to prepare the land for seed sowing. It should be drawn backwards and forwards over the surface of the ground, leaving the land in a fine condition and absolutely level. It should not be used for removing large quantities of small stones. These, if left in the

soil, assist in the drainage and in the movement of air. In the summer they tend to keep the land cool – the surface stones, in fact, act as a mulch. In the winter they can help keep the land warmer. Do not waste time raking land continually just for the purpose of stone removal.

HOEING

Hoes are summer tools; there are two cheap types – the Dutch hoe and the draw hoe, sometimes called a drag or plate hoe. In normal gardens the Dutch hoe is recommended. It should be used between rows of vegetable seedlings to keep down weeds, and everywhere in the garden to provide a dust mulch, if no organic mulches are used. Use a draw hoe for earthing up, or for cutting down large weeds.

A two-pronged hoe known as the Canterbury hoe can be used for earthing up potatoes, to keep the tubers from turning green. It is sometimes necessary to earth up peas, especially autumn-sown ones, before the frosts or cold winds disturb them.

N.B. There is no need to dig. The 8 acre gardens of Arkley Manor, near Barnet have never been dug in the 18 years they have been run by *The Good Gardeners Association*.

Yet, these gardens are very productive and grow beautiful flowers and shrubs as well as all kinds of fruits and vegetables.

Members of *The Good Gardeners Association* are able to visit these gardens at almost any time.

2 Manures and composting

In order to keep up the fertility of the soil it is necessary to add compost regularly. Manures and fertilizers can be grouped into two main sections: (1) organic, and (2) inorganic. Organic manures are the various forms of farmyard manure, poultry manure, composted organic matter, fish manure, meat and bone refuse, shoddy etc. Inorganic fertilizers are chemical manures or 'bag' fertilizers.

The great thing is to build up the humus content of the soil first, and then 'extras' can be added as tonics, if necessary. Plants have to build themselves up both from materials they extract from the air and from the minerals they take up from the soil. It is actually a combination of these two that provides the starches and the sugars that are necessary in plant and crop production.

INORGANIC MANURES

All kinds of minerals necessary to plant growth are found in the soil; about ten are essential. Fortunately for us, six of them are usually present in sufficient quantities in practically every soil, so there are only four that we usually have to apply. These four are: nitrogen, phosphorus, potash and calcium (or, as we commonly apply it, lime). These are known as the macro-nutrients. The micro-nutrients are, for instance, boron, magnesium, manganese, lithium, iron etc. These are supplied by the properly made compost that is applied each season.

Lime is dealt with later on, because it not only supplies plant food, but sweetens up the soil, and for this reason it is usual to talk only about the three macro-nutrients.

All plants require these three particular foods in the correct proportions. It is useless to apply a great quantity of the one in the hope that it will make up for a deficiency of the other. Some plants seem to want more potash than others, while others sometimes require a heavier dressing of nitrogen.

NITROGEN

The main function of nitrogen is to build up the green leaves and stems of the plant. If nitrogen is withheld, the leaves tend to be light green in colour and smaller in size. When nitrogen is applied to growing crops in a quickly available form, the speed at which the plant is growing will increase. An overdose of nitrogen will cause strong, coarse, luxuriant and sappy growth. This makes the plant liable to attacks of fungus diseases, and delays ripening of the crop. Nitrogen, then, is useful for crops where large, succulent green leaves are required, as in the case of cabbages.

PHOSPHORUS
Phosphorus – or phosphates, as components of phosphorus are commonly called – seems to create fruitfulness, and is valuable in increasing root production. Plants starved of phosphorus make little root growth, and therefore suffer during times of drought. If you want to keep your plants growing steadily, firmly, and continuously, then phosphates should help. Further phosphates tend to hasten the ripening of plants.

POTASH
The main value of potash is in the way it tones up a plant. Soils with sufficient potash grow plants with firmer leaves, that are more resistant to disease, and generally hardier. Potash assists in forming strong fibre. With fruit it helps to produce fruits of a better colour which keep longer. The lighter soils are normally deficient in this food. It has been claimed that potash increases the scent in flowering plants.

ORGANIC MANURES
All soils are improved by the regular addition of organic material. What is known as the physical condition is definitely helped by bulky, organic compost. Not only does it supply plant foods, but it adds substances that have the power to act on insoluble compounds in the soil and reduce them to a form that the plant can use. Perhaps the only soil that does not require the addition of organic material is peaty soil, though it will appreciate lime. Heavy soils are improved by organic manuring, which makes them lighter and easier to work. Light soils are made to retain moisture more readily, and so can withstand drought more easily.

FARMYARD MANURE OR DUNG
This is the oldest and perhaps the most popular type of organic

manure, but it is more and more difficult to obtain. It consists of animal excrement, both liquid and solid, and of the litter put down for the animals to lie on. The value of dung varies according to the way the animals have been fed, and according to the way it has been stored. The most valuable farmyard manure is old manure that has been made and kept in a covered-in yard. If manure is left exposed to the action of sun, wind and rain for many months, its value may be reduced by half. Litter can play an important part in altering the value of dung – as, for instance, manure containing straw. Horse manure is more valuable than cow manure, but it loses its value (if kept in the open), more quickly than cow manure. Pig manure is richer in nitrogen, as is sheep manure.

If it can be obtained, and is not expensive, old, properly stored dung should be applied every year. Some land will need heavier dressings; generally, one good barrowload to 10–15 sq. yds is sufficient.

Be careful not to buy dung that has been made with sawdust or wood chippings. The wood is often very harmful.

POULTRY MANURE

Poultry manure should be free from sawdust and disinfectants, and should be stored in a dry place. When applied fresh and wet, its value is halved. It is, however, excellent as an accelerator on the compost heap and should be used at 2 oz to the square yard for every 6-in. layer of refuse collected and trodden level.

PIGEON MANURE

This contains more plant food than poultry manure, and is approximately twice as valuable. It is an excellent activator for the compost heap if used like poultry manure.

FISH MANURE

This is a popular manure, and rightly so. Some firms sell a deodorized type. It is made from waste fish and fish residues, and if the makers have removed the oil it is quite quick-acting. Without any additions it is rich in nitrogen and phosphates, but contains no potash. Some manufacturers do, however, add potash during the process of drying and packing, and then it becomes a complete manure. Fish manure is comparable to all true guanos in that it is able to yield nitrogen to the growing crop throughout the whole season. The analysis of a good fish manure is remarkably constant. The nitrogen varies between 6 and 9 per cent, and the phosphate from 13 to 20 per cent. Fish manure rapidly rots down and feeds the soil. It also stimulates bacterial action.

Some fish manures have other substances added to them to increase their value. The following substances have been found incorporated with first-class fish guanos; dried blood, finely ground hoof and horn, bonemeal and sterilized humus. It is usually applied at 3–4 oz to the square yard.

OTHER ORGANIC FERTILIZERS

Dried blood is not particularly cheap, but is very rich in nitrogen; ground hoof and horn is slow in action, and contains nitrogen and phosphates, but no potash, a normal dressing being 2 oz per square yard. Soot contains nitrogen, and is valuable because it darkens the soil. It contains no phosphates or potash, and is especially useful on heavy soils, making them easier to work and more porous. It is excellent for brussels sprouts in the early summer. Use at 3 oz to the square yard.

BULKY MANURES

SHODDY

This is the waste left behind during the manufacture of various materials. Wool shoddy is more valuable than cotton shoddy, because it contains nitrogen only. All shoddies rot down slowly, and are applied at the rate of, say, one large barrowload to 12 sq. yds. Shoddy is used more often on heavy than on light soils. It is slow in action.

SPENT HOPS

Various kinds of hop manures can be bought. They are quite a good substitute for compost. Normally they contain only a little nitrogen, but no phosphates or potash. A good application is a large barrowload to 10 sq. yds.

SEAWEED

Gardeners who live near the seaside will find rotted seaweed very useful. It is more valuable on the whole than the normal farmyard manure, though it is lower in phosphates. It is, however, much richer in potash. It should be applied at the rate of one large barrowload to 10 sq. yds. It makes an excellent activator for the compost heap.

SEDGE PEAT

This is sold as an alternative to compost. It is not very acid and so can be applied to the land with safety. Apply at the rate of one large bucketful to the square yard and rake in. Be sure <u>not</u> to buy sphagnum peat or moss peat, as it is called. This has very little value as compared with sedge peat.

WOOD ASHES

These are a valuable potash fertilizer. They are about a twelfth as valuable as sulphate of potash, and so very heavy dressings have to be applied if they are to act as a substitute. They are very useful in improving the texture of soils, and because plenty of bonfire ashes are available they are much used in gardens. (Coal ashes can do a great deal of harm and so should be avoided.)

COMPOST AND COMPOST HEAPS

A better organic substance than dung may be made by the gardener with all the vegetable refuse from the house and garden.

THE WOODEN BIN METHOD

Make or obtain a square wooden bin, at least 4 × 4 ft. The planks used to make the bin should have 2-in. spaces in between them to let air in. Treat the wood with a proprietary wood preservative such as Cuprinol or Rentokil. Do not use creosote or tar. Fill the bin to a level of 6 ins with any of the following refuse: potato peelings, tea leaves, dead flowers, rotting leaves, hedge clippings, newspapers etc., plus any litter from rabbit hutches and poultry runs, if you can obtain it.

Tread down well, and level each day. A fish fertilizer or seaweed manure is then sprinkled on at the rate of 3 oz per square yard. Successive layers are made like this as more organic material becomes available.

At the end of 6–7 months (which depends to a certain extent on the material being composed and the time of the year – quicker in spring and summer, slower in winter, the temperature is low) the compost is ripe. It should then be a dark, black, sweet-smelling, powdery substance containing all the macro-nutrients and most of the many micro-nutrients. It should, in addition, contain vitamins, enzymes and anti-biotics. It provides the correct medium for the soil bacteria to work upon, and so plant foods are produced in the right condition and at the right time to be absorbed by the roots and utilized by the plants.

After the first year of composting it is not necessary to add lime as the calcium will have been provided by the plant remains on the heap. Once a week or so, if the weather is dry, the heap may be given a good watering. Take care to keep the heap moist, but not saturated, and when it gets 4 ft high, a fork may be plunged into it perpendicularly in two or three places so as to help aerate it. It is convenient to have two heaps going (say, 4 or 6 × 4 or 6 ft each), one which is almost ready to use and the other which is being piled up to use in six months' time.

The powdery compost should be put on top of the soil in autumn or early winter at the rate of one good barrowload to 10 sq. yds. It may be used at any time, and is ideal for putting on top of the ground as a top dressing or as a mulch along rows of runner beans or peas, as well as all over the soil 1 in. deep where you are growing roses, shrubs, heathers, perennials and the like.

To test the condition of the compost, make a hole with a trowel in the side of the heap. If it is slimy, wet and sour-smelling, strip off the covering and turn the heap, adding drier material plus a sprinkling of lime. If it smells musty, add dilute liquid manure or water, or turn the heap during a rainy period. The compost is ready for use when it has a pleasant, earthy smell and is in a brown, powdery condition.

LIME

When discussing lime previously, we said that the calcium in it was useful as a plant food. This is not the only importance of lime, as it can do a great deal to improve the workability of soils. It can make clay easier to work. It helps to set free other plant foods – particularly potash. It counteracts acidity in the soil. It helps to build up the salts which are used by plants as food, and it is very useful in helping to decompose organic material. Not only does it do all these valuable things, but if it is applied regularly it can prevent attacks of that dreaded disease, clubroot.

Though most plants require lime, there are some that are lime-haters, the most important of which are rhododendrons, azaleas, ericas, gaultherias, kalmias, pieris, several primulas, and several of the gentians.

Some wild plants will only flourish under acid conditions,

and so are taken as indicators of sour soil. These are spurry, sheep's sorrel, corn chrysanthemum and stinking mayweed.

HOW TO APPLY

Lime should be applied on the surface of the ground, and does not need to be dug in. It washes down very quickly, and will easily get to the roots of plants. Unfortunately, this washing away means that applications of lime have to be made regularly to keep land sweet. Never put lime on at the same time as you are applying farmyard manure or any of the acid artificial manures. It is, however, quite safe to dig manures in and then to apply lime on the surface.

TYPES OF LIME

There are three main kinds of lime which can be used, and these are:

(1) *Chalk or limestone*. These may be ground and sold as ground limestone, and contain about half their weight in oxide of lime. Use 5–7 oz per square yard.

(2) *Oxide of lime*. This is sold as quicklime, lump lime and so on. It can also be ground, and is then sold as ground lime. (Please notice the difference between ground limestone and ground lime.) Use 3 oz per square yard.

(3) *Hydrate of lime*. This contains about three-quarters of the amount of oxide of lime as quicklime, though it is very conveniently handled and does not burn. This is the lime that is sold in bags under various proprietary names. Use at 4–6 oz per square yard.

TESTING FOR LIME

It is possible to test soil for acidity and so discover what quantities of lime are needed, if any. Any chemist or seed shop will sell you a small kit containing a green liquid which changes colour according to the amount of lime present.

GREEN MANURING

The idea is to sow a crop purely for the purpose of digging it in shallowly while it is still fresh and green. Various crops are suitable, the commonest being mustard, rye, spinach and tares. If you need to add nitrogen in large quantities, then peas, tares, clover or lupins are sometimes used. It is important to dig the crops in before they get to the flowering stage. They not only add humus to the soil, but help to retain the soluble plant foods which were present when the crop was sown. Such foods may easily be washed away during a rainy period. Directly the ground is free of a crop, one of these green manures can be sown instead of leaving the land bare. Spinach, for instance, is often sown in September and October, and so is rye, while mustard and tares are often sown in April. Mustard has its advantages in that it may be dug in shallowly in less than eight weeks' time; but it has its disadvantages, as it is liable to get clubroot, and so keep this disease going in the ground.

3 Annual and biennial flowers

ANNUALS

Many people believe that it is necessary to spend a lot of money to have a beautiful flowering garden. This is definitely a fallacy, and those who have grown annuals for years will agree with me. But do not forget that the life of an annual is limited to twelve months – so do not expect it to grow up and bloom again year after year.

One of the great advantages of annuals is that they are easy to grow and yet have beautiful flowers, and often scent too, over a long period. Do not just be satisfied with growing the commoner annuals such as nasturtiums, virginia stock, candytuft and cornflower etc., though these can be very beautiful in themselves, but try to grow the annuals that are less well known, but whose names will be found in seed catalogues.

There are two kinds of annuals – the hardy and the half-hardy. Hardy annuals can be sown out of doors either in autumn or in spring, while half-hardy annuals should be raised in frames or under cloches.

SOIL

If you have any choice at all, choose a light soil in preference to a heavy one. Clay soils can be improved by raking in liberally sedge peat and organic material like spent hops or powdery compost. Some plants, like annual larkspur, sweet peas, canary creeper and convolvulus, do well in heavy soils, however.

See that the land is well drained – annuals hate water-logging. Rake in lightly a barrowful of powdery dark brown compost for every 5 sq. yds. It is a good plan to tread the surface level and then rake it over lightly afterwards. This compacts the soil and prevents the seed disappearing into deep crevices. The preparation of a fine tilth before sowing the seed is extremely important.

A good fish manure should be applied to the surface at 3–4 oz to the square yard, and raked in lightly, at least a

26

month before sowing the seed. If it is impossible to do this, give this as a top dressing when the plants are several inches high.

Lime may be given if the ground is acid, but do not forget that there are some plants that dislike lime.

SOWING THE SEED

It is usual to sow annuals in spring, any time from the end of March to the end of April, according to the soil, season and district. Some people, because they live in the north or in an exposed situation, sow seed in frames in the spring and either allow the plants to flower there or transplant them as soon as the weather is better.

If possible autumn sowing is always to be preferred, as the plants grow better and flower much earlier in consequence. In this case the seed is sown any time between mid-August in the north and mid-September in the south. It is not possible to sow all varieties of annuals in this way, as many of them are killed by winter frost, or by damp. For this reason a list of those that normally live through the winter is given on page 29 as a guide to those who wish to take advantage of it.

Cloches are ideal for covering annuals in the winter – in fact, they enable a far greater variety of annuals to be autumn sown.

Sow annuals on a fine, dry day when the soil is in a loose, powdery condition. Sow in rows, a foot apart, in patches or clumps. Be sure not to have clumps too close together. A plant that is going to grow to a foot in height really needs a square foot of space in which to grow to perfection. It is quite a good plan to scratch, with a pointed stick, drifts of varying shapes into which the various kinds of seeds can be sown. Whatever the width of the border, the dwarfer plants should be sown nearer the front and the taller varieties at the back. Occasionally, some of the taller varieties can be allowed to come to the front in order to prevent a monotonous outline.

There is no need to sow deeply or thickly – most of the annual seeds are very small and so they only need to be just covered. Some people mix sand with seed to be sure of sowing them thinly enough. If you do this, use ten times the amount of sand to seed.

After sowing, either rake the bed over, shallowly, or else sift a little soil over through a fine-meshed sieve. Pat the ground lightly with the back of a spade.

THINNING

This is a very important operation which must be done very early. Some people can transplant annuals quite successfully, and some varieties are easier to move than others. As the seed is cheap, this is usually unnecessary, but if you have a miss here and there it is well worhtwhile trying, in order to fill up. Such annuals as cornflowers, calendulas and nigella will usually transplant well.

You may have great difficulty in recognizing the annuals from weeds, especially in their young stage. It is quite easy to pull out all the plants and just leave the weeds there! To help you recognize them, if you are new to the game, why not sow a few seeds in boxes and grow them in a frame, or even on a windowsill indoors, so that they come up a fortnight or so before those outside? Having seen what they are like in the box you will be able to thin those in the garden without any trouble.

If thinning can be done when the soil is moist, so much the better. In dry weather the roots of the little plants you leave in may easily get disturbed and damaged. Thin early, thin rigorously, and thin to a distance of half the height of the plant when fully grown, and you will have good plants that will flower freely.

When annuals are sown in autumn, it is very debatable whether they should be thinned before winter sets in or not. Very often they succeed better if thinning is left until early spring.

STAKING

The great mistake most beginners make is that they do not stake early enough. Another fault is staking with straight, soldier-like sticks such as bamboos. Bamboos are all very well for plants with stiff, strong stems, but for the feathery kinds, and those that branch out, twiggy sticks like pea-sticks are preferable. If you put these in very early, the plants will grow among the twiggy bits and get all the support they need. The twigs are quickly hidden, and the beauty of the plant is not marred. Sunflowers can have a long straight bamboo if you like, and climbers like sweet peas and trapaeolum can clamber up quite tall sticks.

WATERING

Do not water until the plants are well through. Never give

light sprinklings, but soak the ground well either in the evening or early in the morning. Give a mulching of sedge peat or powdery compost all over the soil as soon as the hot weather starts, and this will save both hoeing and watering.

GENERAL CULTIVATION

Hoe the ground continuously to keep it free from weeds unless it has been covered with correctly made compost or sedge peat and then their won't be any weeds. After staking, cutting off dead blooms etc., rake to remove footmarks. Never let the plants go to seed; cut the plant back so that it will throw out new shoots and flower again. People often complain that annuals seem to be coming to their best just as they are going on holiday, and then when they come back the plants seem dead and useless. The tip is to clip the plants back a little, to prevent seeding, the day you go away, so that when you come back the garden is a blaze of colour again.

HARDY ANNUALS

The following is a list of some of the more useful and beautiful annuals:

Name	Height	Colour
Agrostemma	2½ ft	Crimson
Alyssum (sweet)	½ ft	Lilac, white
Asperula	1½ ft	Blue
Bartonia aurea	1 ft	Bright yellow
Calendula	2 ft	Orange, yellow, apricot, golden
Calliopsis	1½ ft	Yellow
Candytuft	1 ft	Crimson, lilac, rose, white
Cornflower	1–3 ft	Blue, purple, rose, white
Erysimum	1½ ft	Yellow, orange
Eschscholtzia (single and double)	1 ft	White, lemon, crimson, orange
Gamolepis tagetes	6 ins	Yellow
Godetia	9 ins–2 ft	Crimson, pink, white
Helichrysum (everlasting)	2½ ft	Orange, yellow, pink, violet, white
Jacobaea	1 ft	Crimson, purple, white
Larkspur	3 ft	Red, white, rose, blue, mauve
Lavatera	4 ft	Pink, white, red
Leptosiphon	6 ins	Purple, lavender

Name	Height	Colour
Limnanthes	6 ins	Yellow, white
Linaria	1 ft	Purple, pink, white, yellow
Linum grandiflorum	1 ft	Blue, red
Love-lies-bleeding	2 ft	Red
Lupins (annual)	2 ft	Blue, white, scarlet, yellow, pink
Mignonette	1 ft	Lilac, white, red
Nasturtium (single and double)	Dwarf and climbing	Yellow, red, rose
Nigella	1½ ft	Blue, white
Oenothera drummondii	1 ft	Yellow
Phacelia	1 ft	Blue
Poppies (all kinds)	2 ft	All colours
Portulaca (single and double)	6 ins	White, crimson, scarlet, primrose
Saponaria	6 ins–2 ft	Pink, white
Scabious	1½ ft	Mauve, yellow, white, red
Silene	9 ins–1½ ft	Rose, pink
Statice (Everlasting)	1½ ft	Blue, rose
Sweet Sultan	1½ ft	Yellow, white, mauve
Ursinia	9 ins	Orange
Viscaria	1 ft	Crimson, pink
Xeranthemum (Everlasting)	2 ft	Purple, white, yellow

Climbers. Convolvulus, Tropaeolum canariense (the canary creeper), nasturtium and sweet peas.

HALF HARDY ANNUALS

In addition to the large group described above, there are a very large number of half-hardy annuals which, with a little care and attention, will make a beautiful show in the summer. The only trouble about them is that they have to be raised in a greenhouse or frame and planted out after all fear of frost is past, say the third week of May.

The following is a list of the more attractive half-hardy annuals:

Name	Height	Colour
Acroclinium (Everlasting)	2 ft	White, rose
Ageratum	1 ft	Blue, white

Antirrhinum	1–2½ ft	White, yellow, pink, red
Arctotis	1 ft	Yellow, mauve, white
Balsam	1½ ft	Rose, scarlet, white
Brachycome	1½ ft	White, mauve, purple, blue
Celosia	2 ft	Crimson, yellow, rose
China Asters	1½–2 ft	Blue, rose, scarlet, pink, white
Cosmos	2½ ft	Pink, white, crimson, mauve
Dimorphotheca	1 ft	Yellow, orange, white
Gilia	1 ft	White, violet, scarlet
Marigold (French and African)	1–2 ft	Lemon, orange, striped
Martynia	2 ft	Mauve
Nemesia	1¼ ft	Blue, carmine, orange, pink, white
Nicotiana (scented)	2½ ft	Red, white
Perilla	1½ ft	Beautiful bronze foliage
Petunia (single and double)	1–2 ft	Various
Phlox drummondii	1¼ ft	Scarlet, white, rose, violet. Yellow, many with a white open eye
Rhodanthe	1 ft	Pink, white
Salpiglossis	2 ft	Various
Schizanthus (single and double)	2 ft	White, pink, red, yellow, variegated
Statice (Everlasting)	2 ft	Mauve, white, yellow
Ten-Week-Stocks	2 ft	All colours
Venidium fastuosum	3 ft	Brilliant orange, dark centre
Verbena	1 ft	Rose, blue, scarlet etc.
Zinnias	3 ft	Crimson, purple, scarlet, sulphur, violet, white, *very* large

Beginners are often worried as to which annuals to use for varying purposes. It may be useful, therefore, to give one or two tables, grouping the plants together under different headings.

Hardy edging plants. Alyssum, asperula, dwarf gilia, dwarf candytuft, kaulfussia, leptosiphon, dwarf nasturtium, nemophila, phacelia, dwarf saponaria, silene, ursinia and virginia stock.

Varieties that can be sown in mid-September. Cornflower, candytuft, calendula, nigella, larkspur (others, like annual chrysanthemum, linaria and sweet sultan may live through the winter).

Annuals suitable for use as cut flowers. Cornflower, candytuft, calendula, nigella, larkspur, clarkia, godetia, gypsophila, linaria, saponaria, sweet sultan.

Annuals for autumn blooming. The following annuals, if sown at the beginning of July, will flower freely at the late end of the year: alyssum, cornflower, candytuft, clarkia, godetia, gypsophila, limnanthes, nasturtium, sweet sultan, virginia stock.

Half-hardy annuals for edging. Ageratum, arcototis, French marigold, nemesia, phlox drummondii, portulaca.

BIENNIALS

The true description of a biennial plant is one which completes its life cycle (ie grows, flowers and seeds) within the second year of germination. When sown one year, they bloom, ripen their seed, and die the following year.

A large number of plants, including canterbury bells, hollyhocks, gaillardias, sweet williams and wallflowers, are really perennials, but are grown as biennials because they do best as such.

Many people have difficulty in recognizing the difference between annuals and biennials, and even confuse them with perennials. Presumably the reason is that many of the annuals seed themselves, and so come up again of their own accord the next year, while some of the perennials are apt to die at the end of the first year, owing to bad treatment.

PREPARATION OF THE SOIL

The ground where biennials are to grow should be raked well and compost added at a bucketful to the square yard. Sedge peat can be used if compost is not available. A fish manure or seaweed manure may be given the following spring, at 3 oz to the square yard.

SOWING THE SEED

The seed of the various biennials is sown during May, June and July. The time of sowing differs according to the type of soil, season and locality. It is usually unnecessary to sow under

A fine stand of maize

Espalier-trained fruit in blossom

Red stemmed sea-kale spinach

Winter flowering heaths etc.

glass; shallow drills can be drawn out 1 ft apart on friable soil, and the seed sown in these.

Plant firmly, allowing 1 ft or so between the plants except for hollyhocks, when 4 ft must be allowed. As a general rule the earlier sowing outside is preferable to the later sowing. As soon as the plants are 3 ins high they are planted out into further prepared ground or put into permanent beds or borders.

LIST OF BIENNIALS

Name	Height	Colour
Brompton stocks	2 ft	Violet, yellow, rose, pink, mauve, white
Canterbury bells (single and double)	2½ ft	Blue, mauve, rose, white
Foxglove	2–6 ft	Mauve, white
Gilia	1 ft	Scarlet
Hollyhock	6–8 ft	Red, pink, yellow, flame
Honesty	2 ft	Purple, white
Pentstemon	2½ ft	Red, pink, purple
Poppy, Sunbeam and Iceland (single and double)	1 ft	Orange, yellow, white
Sweet rocket	2 ft	Purple, white
Sweet William	2 ft	Various
Wallflower	1 ft	Brown, yellow, red, orange, white, mixed

Antirrhinums and Pentstemons are often treated as biennials as well.

4 Perennials and herbacious borders

Of all the plants that are grown in the garden the perennial is usually the most popular, because it comes up year after year. This term (strictly speaking) refers not only to herbaceous perennials, but also to trees and shrubs. This chapter, however, will deal with herbaceous perennials only.

Herbaceous perennials can be bought to suit all tastes. They produce flowers of all colours, and can be planted to keep up a supply of blooms from, say, April until October. Many of the perennials stand dry periods far better than annuals, and on the whole they are stronger and sturdier. Like annuals, they can be grown purely for cutting, or can be planted in a border (often known as a herbaceous border).

PROPAGATION

Perennials can be propagated in various ways: (1) by sowing seeds, (2) by root cuttings, (3) by division, and (4) by stem cuttings.

SEED SOWING

The seeds are sown either in the open in a sheltered place, or in a cold frame, about the beginning of June. It is an advantage if the soil is on the light side, so if you have heavy land try to dig in some sand to lighten it.

Shallow drills, $\frac{1}{4}$ in. deep, are taken out 6 ins apart; sow the seed thinly in them. If the weather be dry, and the soil too, it is a good plan to water the bed well the afternoon before sowing. Try to raise sturdy seedlings by sowing thinly to obviate thinning later. Having sown the seed, rake the ground over lightly, making certain to rake in the same direction as the drill, so you do not disturb the seed in the rows. It may be necessary, after sowing, to water through a fine rose.

If the seeds are sown in a frame, keep it closed down until the young plants are through, when some ventilation may be done. Continue the ventilation whenever the weather is warm enough, but if it is too bright and sunny, shade the frames by

34

putting whitewash on the glass or cover them over with sacking or nylon netting.

There is always a danger when sowing seed outside that young seedlings may be damaged by birds and insects. Prevent bird damage by putting in little bamboos at fixed intervals and stretching black cotton in zigzag fashion in between them. To ward off insects spray regularly with Derris.

As soon as the plants are 3 ins high – and this may be within a month or six weeks of the time of seed sowing – they can be planted into their permanent position. (This, however, is not usual. They are generally transplanted into other beds 9 ins or so square, to grow on until big enough to use in the herbaceous border.) The new bed should be lightly forked and sedge peat or powdery brown compost incorporated in the top 2–3 ins at one bucketful to 5 sq. yds.

Sandy soils should have a good fish manure added at the rate of 4 oz to the square yard, and many people use bonemeal at the rate of 2 oz per square yard in addition. These are raked in some time before the plants are put out.

Do not plant carelessly. Spread the roots out evenly, give them plenty of room, and firm them. It is dangerous to make a rough hole with a dibber, for the result too often is that an air pocket is left underneath the plant. When the plants are all set, give the bed a good soaking from a large watering can. This bed will need hoeing throughout the growing season so that the plants will not be retarded by weeds.

The transplanted perennials will be ready to put out into their permanent positions in the autumn of the second season.

ROOT CUTTINGS

There are many varieties of perennials that do not come true from seed. For this reason it is necessary to adopt other methods, and a favourite one is the root cutting. A much larger number of plants can be raised from the original, as the roots are cut up into quite small portions, each one of which will make a plant. Unfortunately it is only the plants with fleshy roots that respond well to such treatment. The most popular example is anchusa, though others, like delphiniums and lupins, are also propagated in this way.

The plants are dug up very carefully immediately after flowering. The roots are then cut into portions 3 ins long. Make a square cut at the top end and a slanting one at the bottom end. This enables the gardener to know for certain, after the cuttings have been prepared, which way up the planting ought to be done. It is no good planting roots upside-down!

The root cuttings are placed in sandy soil (some people use coarse silver sand alone), each cutting being 2–3 ins away from its neighbour, and, if in rows, these may be 4–6 ins apart. Position them so that they are covered with not more than ½ in. of sand.

Root cuttings may be inserted in pots, which can be placed in a frame or in a cool greenhouse. More often the root cuttings are placed direct into sandy compost in a cool frame.

The young plants that result can be planted out the following spring.

DIVISION

Perhaps the easiest method of all is to divide the plants into two or more portions when they are large enough. Those with fibrous roots like the pyrethrum are propagated most easily in this way. You can lay the plant on the ground and chop it up into suitable sizes by means of a sharp spade. A better method with other plants is to insert two forks back to back into the centre of the clump, and then, by forcing the handles apart, gently but firmly, break it into two pieces. In the case of very large clumps that have been growing for several years the outer portions (being younger than the centre part) should be retained and the central (or original) plant thrown away. This is done in the autumn. The clumps should be lifted with as much soil attached to the roots as possible, and, after division, the selected portions should be replanted immediately. Some plants, like chrysanthemum maximum, should be divided in this way every three years, and michaelmas daisies every year. Other plants, like lupins, paeonies and Japanese anemones, hate disturbance, and are best left alone for as long as possible.

CUTTINGS

There is yet another method of propagation ie cuttings. Young side shoots, often with roots attached to them, may be severed from their parent plants in the autumn, and transplanted into a specially prepared bed. Green cuttings of perennials such as scabious may be severed from the plants early in the summer and planted out to strike into a sandy compost in a frame.

Disbudding chrysanthemums

TIPS FOR PERENNIALS

Some plants will need special treatment – for instance, the scabious likes a handful of lime put over each plant before the winter sets in. Delphiniums have coal ashes put round them towards the end of the autumn, to keep the stems from rotting off, as well as keeping slugs at bay.

Never let the flowers seed, so cut off the flower heads regularly and as a result, with varieties that flower early, a second crop of blooms often results.

Stake the taller varieties early enough to ensure straight stems. Use a bamboo or two, placed firmly in the centre or at the sides of the clump to keep the stems upright. Pea-sticks are often used, especially in the herbaceous border, as advised for annuals.

The use of sedge peat or home-made brown powdery compost as a mulch is recommended, especially for perennials like helenium, phlox and trollius, which often suffer during dry periods.

When planted out for cut-flower purposes, give the plants plenty of room for development; this means that the rows will have to be 18 ins apart, and the plants 1 ft apart in the rows. Hoeing will have to be carried out throughout the summer, to keep down weeds and to produce a dust mulch. The alternative, of course, is to apply sedge peat in between the rows at a 1-in. depth.

TYPES AND VARIETIES

There are hundreds of herbaceous plants, and I can only attempt to give quite a brief list. To make it easier for readers to plant out borders, I have tried dividing those I have chosen into colour groups.

Name	Soil	Height	Propagation	Time of flowering	Position
ORANGE AND YELLOWS					
Alstroemeria	Light	2 ft	Seeds and division	July	Sunny
Bocconia	Moist	5 ft	Division	July	,,
Centaurea	Average	3–5 ft	,,	June–July	,,
Coreopsis	,,	2 ft	Seeds	July–Aug	Sunny or shady
Doronicum	,,	2 ft	Division	April	Sunny
Gaillardia	,,	3 ft	Seeds and division	Aug	,,
Geum	,,	2 ft	Seeds	May–Aug	Sunny or semi-shady
Helenium	,,	4 ft	Division	July, Aug, Sept	,,
Helianthemum	,,	9 ins	Seeds and cuttings	June	,,
Helianthus	Light	6 ft	Seeds and division	Sept–Oct	Sunny
Oenothera	Average	2 ft	Division	June–July	,,
Rudbeckia	,,	4–6 ft	,,	Aug	Sunny or shady
Solidago	,,	4 ft	,,	Sept	Semi-shady
Thermopsis	,,	2 ft	,,	June–July	Sunny
Verbascum	,,	5 ft	,,	June–July	,,
BLUES					
Aconitum	Average	4 ft	Division	July–Aug	Sunny or shady
Anchusa	,,	4 ft	Division and root cuttings	June–July	Sunny
Delphinium	,,	5 ft	Seeds and division	June–July	,,
Echinops	,,	3 ft	Division	Aug	,,
Erigeron	,,	1½ ft	,,	June–Aug	,,
Eryngium	,,	3 ft	,,	July–Aug	,,
Iris	,,	1½ ft	,,	June–Aug	,,
Mertensia	,,	1 ft	,,		Semi-shady
Nepeta	,,	1 ft	Division and cuttings	June–July	Sunny
Salvia azurea	,,	2 ft	Division	July–Aug	,,
Scabious	,,	2½ ft	,,	July–Aug	,,
Veronica	,,	1 ft	,,	April–May	,,
Vinca	,,	1 ft	,,	May	Shady

RED

Name	Soil	Height	Propagation	Month	Position
Dielytra	Average	2 ft	Division	May–June	Semi-shady
Geum	,,	2 ft	Seeds	May–Aug	,,
Lychnis chalcedonia	,,	2 ft	Seeds and division	July–Aug	Sunny
Monarda	,,	2 ft	Division	June–July	,,
Poppy oriental	,,	3 ft	Seeds and division	May–June	,,

WHITE

Name	Soil	Height	Propagation	Month	Position
Achillea White Pearl	Average	2 ft	Division	June–July	Sunny or semi-shady
Anemone Japonica	,,	4 ft	,,	Sept	Shady
Gypsophila	,,	3 ft	Seeds, grafting	July	Sunny
Helleborus	Heavy, rich	1½ ft	Division	Dec	Semi-shady
Lilies	Average	3 ft	Bulbs	June	Sunny or semi-shady
Phlox	Moist	4 ft	Division and cuttings	Aug–Aept	Semi-shady

MAUVE AND PURPLE

Name	Soil	Height	Propagation	Month	Position
Betonica	Average	2 ft	Division	July–Aug	Sunny
Galega	,,	4 ft	,,	May–June	Sunny or shady
Stachys	,,	1 ft	,,	May–June	,,
Campanula	,,	2½ ft	,,	June–Aug	,,
Centaura dealbata	,,	3 ft	,,		,,

PINK

Name	Soil	Height	Propagation	Month	Position
Armeria	Light	6 ins	Division	June	Sunny
Phlox	Moist	4 ft	Cuttings	Aug–Sept	Semi-shady
Potentilla	Average	2 ft	Division	June–July	Sunny
Sedum spectabile	Moist	1 ft	,,	Aug–Sept	Semi-shady
Sidalcea	Average	1 ft	,,	July–Aug	Sunny

MIXED COLOURS

Name	Soil	Height	Propagation	Month	Position
Aquilegia	Average	3 ft	Seeds and division	April–July	Semi-shady
Campanula	,,	2–4 ft	,, ,,	June–July	Sunny or semi-shady
Foxglove	,,	4 ft	Seeds	June–July	Semi-shady
Hollyhock	,,	10 ft	,,	July–Sept	Sunny
Lupin	,,	3 ft	Seeds and division	May–June	,,
Paeony	Heavy, rich	2 ft	Division	May–June	Sunny or semi-shady
Phlox	,,	2 ft	Division and cuttings	July–Aug	,,
Pyrethrum	Average	2 ft	Division	May–June	Sunny
Thalictrum	,,	2–3 ft	,,	June–July	,,

HERBACEOUS BORDERS

We have already discussed the way the ground should be prepared and the types of plants that can be grown. So all that has to be done now is to discuss the methods of planting and good colour schemes.

Aim to make the border look as natural as possible, so do not plant in rows. Try to have four or five plants in a group, but in a small border three plants will do. These groups should be irregular in shape, some of them perhaps actually merging into the taller groups behind. I like to think of them as drifts, some of the groups drifting into and even past another set of plants of a different type growing behind them. If you make these drifts irregular in shape they can sweep round each other and prevent that stiff, artificial look.

Do not make it an inviolate rule to have all the largest plants at the back and all the dwarf ones in the front. Keep to this idea in a general way, but occasionally bring taller plants to the front so as to break up the view and prevent monotony. This creates new vistas as you walk along the outside of the border.

Do not place all the earlier flowering plants in the front of the border, otherwise as soon as they have finished blooming this part will look bare and unsightly. If, on the other hand, these plants are towards the centre of the border, it is possible to plant groups that bloom, say, in September in front of them, so that they hide the fading stems of the central group. Do not plant all the early blossoming varieties at one end of the border and those that flower later on at the other end. Try and distribute the blossoming period right over the border as a whole, to achieve a colourful effect all through it during spring, summer and early autumn.

BORDERS OF ONE COLOUR

Most people have a favourite colour, and you might like to have a blue border, a yellow border, and so on. This is quite possible, and you can find out a larger number of perennials (in particular colours you require) than those given in my list. You can extend this idea, if you like, into borders of two or three colours only. For instance, a blue and grey border is rather fascinating, and, if you like bright colours, why not give a border of yellows, oranges and reds alone a try?

PERIOD BORDERS

If you have a big garden, you may want to plant out one or

two borders to flower during particular months of the year.
It is not usual to aim at much more than a spring border
and an autumn border. The latter could consist entirely of
varieties of michaelmas daisies, with perhaps some chrysanthemums. It is nice to have a border of this kind to which you can
go for inspiration during the duller months of the year. And if,
for instance, you are always away on holiday in August, you
may want to miss out the plants that bloom during that month.

ASPECT BORDERS

Some parts of your garden will be sunny, others may well be
shady. By using the plants that like shade you can have quite
a pleasing border in such a position. Even in the general border
there may be sunnier and shadier areas, and care should be
taken to plant these up with varieties that thrive best under
such conditions.

NARROW BORDERS

In a small garden it is often impossible to have the 12-ft- or
even 6-ft-wide borders that are normally recommended for
herbaceous borders. Use plants that are not too tall. There are
plenty of attractive flowering plants of this character, both
feathery and solid, for instance heuchera, salvia virgata
nemorosa, bergamot, blue flax, flag iris, montbretia, phlox,
the perennial cornflower (centaurea) and so on. There are
other plants that do quite well as edgings: the pinks, lambs'
tongues (stachys), thrift (armeria), various veronicas, violas,
and even our old friend London pride.

GENERAL HERBACEOUS BORDERS

In this wide border plan out a scheme so that all colours, all
shapes and all sizes are grouped together in an interesting
arrangement. Design the border to look bright from, say, May
until October by using plants of varying heights, blossoming
at different times.

Take care with colour; it is not a good plan to have puce
pinks fighting with the reds – though most colours blend
better with one another in the open than they do indoors.

If in your drifts you can arrange for one colour, say light
blue, to drift into a deeper coloured blue and finally to merge
into another group of plants, taller and of another type of blue,
so much the better. These drifts of colour planned in this way
are very effective. You want great splashes of colour and not

little spots here and there. Some plants have more scent than others, and it is quite a good plan to include these. Scent in a garden is practically a necessity, and the paeony, monarda, and lemon-scented verbena are examples of those which add a pleasant perfume to their surroundings.

BACKGROUNDS

It is a good plan to have dark green background to the herbaceous border. Most flowering plants look well against green, and actually a border planted with a lawn as a background is quite a good idea. Another plan is to have an evergreen hedge as background – the yew is often used for this purpose, but lonicera or cupressus will do just as well. A fence of cordon fruit trees can be used, especially if space is restricted, while flowering shrubs and climbing rose pillars are quite useful.

These should not be where they will cast shade on the border, and so should normally be on the north side. Taller specimens that are quite suitable are flowering crabs, laburnums and prunus, while small trees with pleasant foliage tints include the maple, barberis, dogwood and euonymus. There is no need for these to be in a straight line.

SUPPORTS

In the case of bushy types of flowers, pea-sticks should be used. These should be placed in and around each clump of flowers to allow the stems and foliage to grow up among them; the supports are hidden and yet provide exactly what is needed, and the natural shape of the plant is retained. Staking must begin as early as May. Individual bamboos or stakes may be used for the flower stems of the taller varieties such as delphiniums, and these should reach nearly, but not quite up to, the flowers. Ties should be made in two or more places to keep the stems at the right angle.

MANAGEMENT

In the spring, as the young shoots start to grow, take care to protect them from pests like slugs – use Draza pellets. As the warmer weather starts, mulching with sedge peat 1 in. deep all over the ground will prevent slugs from moving about. Lighter soils need this mulch more than heavier ones.

Continue hoeing throughout the summer if sedge peat or compost mulching has not been done, and, if it is difficult to get in between some groups, use a small hand fork.

In extremely dry weather the border can be flooded. Overhead irrigation is effective to freshen up a border. This should be done in the evening.

Go over the border regularly and remove dying and dead blooms. This will not only improve the look of the border, but will enable the plants to flower more freely. As they die down, the stems of the plants should be cut with a sharp knife to within 3 ins of the ground, and when autumn comes the dead leaves and rubbish may be cleared away. If this presents you from seeing clearly where the clumps are, little bamboo sticks may be pushed into the ground to mark the positions.

After frost it may be necessary to go over the border and firm some plants in. Aquilegias have a nasty habit of rising out of the ground, as do geums.

The mulching with properly made compost or sedge peat will control the annual weeds. Thus no hoeing is necessary. The top dressing prevents the weed seeds from germinating. The worms will pull in what is needed to build up the humus content of the soil.

5 Bulbs

Beautiful spring shows can be created with bulbs. They have a very large choice of both variety and colour. The flowering period goes on for a very long time: there is no reason at all, for instance, why your early show of flowers should not start at the beginning of March and continue until the beginning of June.

It is wasteful to consider bulbs as annuals. Too many gardeners plant them, let them flower, and then dig the bulbs up and throw them away. In many soils bulbs will increase, and if you compost the ground well before you plant them, and are careful to remove just the flower heads before they go to seed, the bulbs will build up little bulblets at their sides. To obtain this increase of bulbs you must allow the plant to grow naturally. Make certain that all the food in the leaves is passed back to the bulb. Do this by not cutting off the foliage until it has turned brown and died away.

In a year or two's time the bulblets can be severed from their parents and planted out in another position. They themselves, in a year or two's time, will grow into full-sized bulbs and flower well.

There is no need to leave the bulbs in the place in which they were flowering right until the time of dying down if you wish to put other plants in their place. They can be dug up and heeled in in an odd part of the garden, to allow the leaves to pass back their food undisturbed.

Many bulbs, like daffodils, are quite happy when planted out in grass, and will go on growing there for years undisturbed. They will increase all the time, and for quite a small outlay you can have a 100 per cent interest of beauty for many years.

DAFFODIL
This is one of the largest group of bulbous flowers; it is classified as narcissi.

PLANTING
Most types of daffodils like a warm, well-drained soil, with the

exception perhaps, of the poeticus group, which like a heavier soil. Plant early in autumn, the larger bulbs deeper than the smaller ones. It is quite a good plan to plant bulbs at a depth equal to three times their own width.

VARIETIES

There are a very large number of varieties in each main section, but the following, which I have chosen at random, do very well in an ordinary garden: Scarlet Elegance, Emperor, Golden Harvest, Horace, Sir Carlton, Watkin, Fortune, King Alfred, Beersheba, St Ives, Adjutant, Bonfire, Cheerfulness, Rembrandt, Delightful.

TULIP

As with daffodils, there are various divisions of tulip varieties. For instance, there are single earliest, cottage tulips, darwins for later on, and so on. In each division there is a very large number of varieties.

PLANTING

Tulips do not do well in grass, but they can, on the other hand, be left in cultivated borders of the garden, undisturbed, for a number of years. On the whole they do best on heavier soils, and they seem to like lime. Many people make the mistake of not planting tulip bulbs deep enough, and to avoid tulip fire, a bad disease, planting 9 ins deep is advisable.

Planting should be done in early autumn, and the final lifting and drying of the bulbs, if this is desired, should not be done until the middle of July. To get the best results from tulips, the ground should be given a good dressing of well prepared compost.

VARIETIES

Again it is impossible to give lists of varieties and descriptions, but I will mention a few, again taken at random, that I know will do well under ordinary garden conditions.

Single Earlies. Couleur Cardinal, Mon Tresor, Keizerskroon, Prince of Austria, Sunburst.

Cottage Tulips. Carrara, Inglescombe Yellow, Inglescombe Pink, John Ruskin, Princess Margaret Rose, Golden Harvest.

Darwin Tulips. Clara Butt, Pride of Haarlem, Princess Elizabeth, Bartigon, Apeldoorn, Holland's Glory, Aristocrat, Orange Wonder, Queen of the Night, Paris.

HYACINTH

Hyacinths are divided up into various sections, the principal ones being the Roman and Dutch. They are grown a lot in pots for indoors, and they are perhaps the most suitable of all bulbs for this purpose. They can, however, be grown out of doors, and whole beds of these, of different colours, are very fascinating indeed.

PLANTING

They are usually planted in holes 2–3 ins deep and 6 ins apart. On the whole they like a light soil rather than a heavy one.

VARIETIES

The following are quite good varieties for out of doors.

Blue. Marie, Blue Giant, Bismarck, Delft's Blue.

Pinks and reds. Lady Derby, Pink Pear, Anne Marie, Jan Bos.

White. L'Innocence, Snow Queen, Carnegie.

Yellow. Prince Henry, Yellow Hammer.

CROCUS

These are used a lot as edgings for borders or for planting in grass, where they look very natural. They are useful in a rockery too, for spring colour.

PLANTING

They should be planted 2 ins deep, and at least 2 ins apart.

VARIETIES

Some good varieties are Golden Yellow, Yellow Mammoth and Queen of the Blues, Snowstorm (pure white), Amethyst (soft lavender), Striped Beauty (striped lilac).

CHIONODOXA

PLANTING

This charming little flower, also known as Glory of the Snow, should be planted in clumps of at least six or more, allowing each bulb 1½ ins each way. Plant them 2 ins deep, and they will flower freely and give a regular sheaf of blue very early in the spring.

Bulbs for February flowers

IRIS

I have heard irises described as 'the poor man's orchid', and certainly they are quite cheap to grow. They are beautiful as border flowers, and as cut flowers they can hardly be surpassed. The Dutch iris flowers towards the end of May. The Spanish iris flowers towards the beginning of June, and the English iris late in June.

PLANTING

They are usually planted 3 ins deep, and about 5 ins apart.

VARIETIES

The following are the varieties I would recommend.

Dutch iris. Imperator (27 ins), large, brilliant blue; Wedgwood (24 ins), pale blue; King Mauve, deep mauve; Lemon Queen, bright citron yellow.

Spanish iris. Cajanus (26 ins), large flower, bright canary yellow; Queen Wilhelmina (20 ins), pure white; King of Blues (20 ins), rich deep blue.

English iris. Prince of Wales (18 ins), dark blue; Blue Celeste (22 ins), sky blue.

MUSCARI (GRAPE HYACINTH)
These only grow about 8 ins high, and can be grown in the border, rockery, or in grass. They prefer slight shade.

PLANTING
It is usual to plant them in clumps 3 ins deep.

SCILLA
These are planted in a similar way to muscari and are very early flowering. Plant most varieties 2 ins deep, but campanulata and nutans 3 ins deep. These two latter do well under trees and in borders. The ordinary scilla is siberica, and this has bright flowers which come out at the same time as the snowdrop.

WINTER ACONITE
These flower in February, and grow well in shady and moist situations. They look well under trees, and do well in grassland. Cilicica grows 4 ins high, and hyemalis 3 ins high. Both bear yellow flowers.

SNOWDROP
These are charming when planted in grass, or even in a border. The giant single snowdrop grows 9–12 ins high; its correct name is galanthus elwesii. G. nivalis is the ordinary variety, which grows 6 ins high.

PLANTING
Plant the bulbs 3 ins deep.

6 Shrubs and hedges

SHRUBS

Large numbers of beautiful flowering shrubs can be purchased, and they should be used whenever possible in place of the commonplace evergreens. Shrubs have their uses, as they can be grown for different purposes. For instance they make a good background for a herbaceous border. They provide shelter. They give large splashes of colour to a height often unattainable by the herbaceous plant.

There is such a large selection of hardy flowering shrubs today that there are indeed enough varieties to suit all soils and gardens.

BUYING SHRUBS

Don't forget to purchase the shrubs from a first-class nursery that specializes in them. Get flowering shrubs sent to you early in November, and evergreens even earlier than this – say early in October. When the shrubs arrive all the damaged roots should be cut carefully away with the cut pointing upwards. Remember that, if you are buying berry-bearing shrubs whose flowers are unisexual (that is to say the male and female flowers are borne on different pods), you should order plants of both sexes, because the female plant will only bear berries when a male plant is nearby. A typical example is the holly.

In addition to shrubs that flower at different times (see lists), there are those that have coloured stems in winter; those which have beautiful autumn colouring (there is a long list of these); those that have handsome berries and fruits; and those that have lovely foliage. Some will do quite well in a windy place. Others like a poor, dry, sandy soil. Some do well on a very chalky soil, while others thrive in moist boggy districts.

PLANNING THE SHRUB BORDER

Plant in groups in the same way as suggested for herbaceous borders. Even in narrow borders avoid having only two rows of shrubs, by planting some of the smaller growing varieties in groups of three or four, with an occasional large or tall shrub

49

to give height and variation. Shrub borders always look sparsely planted if the back shrub is placed directly behind the one in the front row.

Do not plant close together shrubs bearing flowers of colours which obviously clash. Try to arrange that the period of blooming is spread right the way through the border – for instance, don't have one end of the border in a blaze in the spring, and then looking dull for the rest of the year, while the other end is only at its best in the autumn. Distribute the flowering periods of the shrubs evenly throughout. Even in quite small borders see that you have some colour for most months of the year.

Think about the height to which the various shrubs will grow, and the amount of room they will take up when fully grown. Remember that some shrubs will creep along the ground, while others will stand up straight.

You can arrange to fill up the spaces between your shrubs in the first few years by sowing annuals, by planting out wallflowers and the like, or by putting in one or two herbaceous plants as a temporary measure.

In order to get height in the shrubbery, it is possible to use flowering trees like prunus, mountain ash or laburnum, and some people like to have pillars of rambler roses.

PREPARATION OF THE BORDER

Fork the ground all over very shallowly, giving at the same time a liberal dressing of properly prepared compost. If the soil is heavy, lighten it by adding dry, powdery sedge peat; and, if sandy, well-rotted compost can be incorporated to help conserve the moisture. Remember that you can plant shrubs to suit either kind of soil. Mulching well with compost will help the shrubs to grow away freely and so get established early. Whatever is done, take care to see that all the perennial weeds are eliminated during this initial preparation.

Lime. Many shrubs appreciate a dressing of lime, but azaleas, rhododendrons, heaths and kalmias (peat-loving plants) should never have lime given to them in any form.

Manuring. Every year it may be necessary to give the shrubs an extra mulching of compost or sedge peat early in May. All soils will appreciate a dressing of fish manure at 3 oz to the square yard in the spring. The main compost or sedge peat dressing should be applied in the late autumn. Never fork among the shrubs, which might do damage to the roots.

GENERAL CULTIVATION

Keep the ground where the shrubs are being grown free from
weeds; the 1-in.-deep mulching will do this automatically.
Plant the trees firmly in the first place, and then keep them
firm by staking if necessary. Do not tie the stake directly to the
stem of the shrub, which can easily be injured, but wrap a piece
of sacking round the stem first. Use tarred string when tying,
and be sure to untie in October of every year and tie up again.

PLANTING

Deciduous shrubs can be transplanted any time from September to May. October and November are usually preferable,
but February and March are quite suitable. The months of
April and May are suitable for evergreen shrubs such as hollies
and rhododendrons.

Dig a hole sufficiently large to take all the roots of the shrub
without having to bend them back. Prune the damaged roots
with a sharp knife so that the cut faces the ground when the

Planting conifers. Note the soil at the side put on to sacking so as not to
spoil the lawn

bush is planted. Do not plant any deeper than the soil mark seen on the stem. Plant when the soil is in a nice friable condition, and not during wet periods or frost. Late planting often means that the shrubs have great difficulty in living through a hot summer, and will need regular soakings of water during drought.

PRUNING

Pruning should only be done if it is really necessary. Do not prune unless you have to, and be quite sure you are doing the right thing at the right time.

In the first place, there is simple pruning, which can be carried out every winter. This consists of cutting out the dead or dying branches, removing very weak wood and thinning out where the branches are obviously overcrowded.

A good general rule is that shrubs should be pruned just after the flowers fade. There are, for instance, shrubs that flower early in the year (many of them on walls), on wood made the previous summer. These obviously should be pruned after flowering, and this leaves a full season in which further flowering branches can be produced. The following are typical examples: flowering currants, forsythias, prunus triloba, and the following spiraeas: S. arguta, S. prunifolia, S. canecens, and S. thunbergii.

There are large numbers of evergreen shrubs that are pruned merely by having the awkward and straggling shoots shortened to make a more shapely bush. Examples are rhododendrons, choisya, buddleia globosa and several of the berberis.

Some shrubs have to be thinned back hard if they are too tall, and the lower and shorter branches may, of course, then be left unpruned. Deutzias, weigelas, the snowball tree or guelder roses are examples of this.

Most people are fond of lilac, which tends to grow tall very quickly. To keep lilacs small, some of the branches may be cut back in June, the weak shoots being pruned back hard also. Remove all the growths coming up directly from the roots (these are known as suckers), as they will rob the bush of food etc. and will make cultivation difficult.

Then there are the shrubs which flower on the young wood made that year. These are cut back during the early spring, some, like the buddleia variabilis, being pruned back really hard.

Other examples of similar treatment, though perhaps not

A Buddleia variabilis after its yearly pruning

quite so drastic, are colutea, honeysuckles, ceanothus azureus, C. Gloire de Versailles, jasminum officinale, and so on.

Whatever pruning is done, be sure to use a sharp knife or a very sharp pair of secateurs; large wounds should be cleaned up and made smooth, to be painted over afterwards with thick white lead paint.

Tidying. Some shrubs, like azaleas and rhododendrons, tend to form seeds directly the flowers have faded. Remove all faded flowers immediately they are seen; in this way you will not only improve the appearance of the plants, but you will help them too.

HARDY SHRUBS FOR VARIOUS NEEDS
It is impossible to give a complete list of all the shrubs one could grow. Below are a number of shrubs that are easy to grow and will give plenty of colour.

Putting shrub cuttings of various kinds into a cold frame

Flowering shrubs and trees

Berberis darwinii	April	Yellow	8 ft
Berberis stenophylla	May	Yellow	8 ft
Buddleia globosa	June	Orange	10 ft
Buddleia variabilis	July	Mauve	10 ft
Cistus in variety	June–Aug	White, pink	2–5 ft
Crataegus oxyacantha (scarlet thorn)	May–June	Red	15 ft
Cytisus in variety	May	White, yellow, red	6 ft
Deutzia gracilis	June	White	3 ft
Deutzia kalmiaflora	June	Pink	4 ft
Diervilla	May–June	Pink	5 ft
Escallonia macrantha	June–Nov	Pink	5 ft
Forsythia spectabilis	March	Yellow	8 ft
Genista hispanica	May–June	Yellow	3 ft
Hamamelis mollis	Jan	Yellow	10 ft

Kerria japonica	April	Yellow	6 ft
Lilac (see syringa)			
Olearia haastii	June	White	5 ft
Philadelphus	June-July	White	2–8 ft
Rhododendron	May	White, red, mauve	2–10 ft
Ribes sanguineum	April	Pink	7 ft
Rosemary	April–May	Mauve	5 ft
Spiraea Anthony Waterer	June–Sept	Pink	2 ft
Spiraea arguta	April–May	White	8 ft
Spiraea confusa	May	White	8 ft
Syringa (lilac)	May–June	White, purple	12 ft
Ulex europaeus	April–May	Yellow	5 ft
Viburnum opulus	June	White	9 ft
Viburnum tinus	Dec–March	White	8 ft

Autumn-tinted shrubs and trees. Acer japonicum, Berberis aggregata pratii, Berberis thunbergii, Berberis wilsonae, Crataegus prunifolia, Rhus typhina, Spirae thunbergii, Viburnum lantana.

Berried and fruiting shrubs. Berberis aggregata, Berberis gagnepainii, Berberis polyantha, Berberis verruculosa, Colutea arborescens, Cotoneaster (all varieties), Cydonia maulei, Pyracantha, Pyrus baccata, Pyrus malus, Rosa moyesii, Sambucus, Skimmia japonica, Symphoricarpus, Viburnum lantana.

Catkin-bearing shrubs. Alnus glutinosa, Betula nigra, Garrya elliptica, Populus tremulus, Salix caprea.

Coloured stems and bark. Betula alba verrucosa, Cornus alba sibirica, Kerria japonica, Rubus biflorus, Salix vitellina, Salix vitellina britzensis.

Lime-hating shrubs. Andromeda, Azalea, Erica, Kalmia, Pernettya, Rhododendron, Vaccinium.

Shrubs for shade. Berberis aquifolium (mahonia), Eyonymus japonica, Leycesteria formosa, Ruscus aculeatus, Symphoricarpus, Vinca.

Shrubs for walls

South. Actinidia chinensis, Aristolochia sipho, Bignonia capriolata, Caenothus dentatus, Caenothus Gloire de Versailles, Clematis, Eccremocarpus scaber, Jasminum primulinum, Jasminum revolutum, Magnolia grandiflora, Solanum crispum, Solanum jasminoides, Veronica hulkeana, Vitis heterophylla.

West. Bignonia capreolata, Ceanothus rigidus, Chimonanthus fragrans, Clematis, Cydonia japonica, Forsythia suspensa, Pyracantha augustifolia, Rambler roses.

East. Cotoneaster simonsii, Cotoneaster horizontalis, Garrya elliptica, Jasminum nudiflorum, Pyracantha, Vitis inconstans veitchii (ampelopsis).

North. Cotoneaster horizontalis, Cotoneaster simonsii, Garrya elliptica, Hedera, Jasminum nudiflorum, Polygonum baldschuanicum.

HEDGES

Before planting a hedge think whether it is really necessary. Remember that it can be used for three purposes, and three purposes only: (1) to form an impenetrable boundary, (2) to act as a division in the garden or as a background for plants, (3) to provide a shelter or windbreak. If you want an impenetrable boundary you will have to plant a hedge of a spiky nature such as holly, myrobolan plum, buckthorn, blackthorn, hawthorn or quick, but for the other two purposes there is a much wider choice.

A hedge planted as a division or background must be kept within its alloted limits and should always be as attractive as possible. Don't plant a privet or a laurel for this purpose. They are far too uninteresting and commonplace. Think of hedging plants such as lonicera nidita, berberis, cotoneaster, escallonia or, if you like dark browns, beech or hornbeam. If the garden is by the seaside, or in fact anywhere within ten or fifteen miles of the sea, I can well recommend tamarisk, sea buckthorn and atriplex halimus. The latter will even grow well in pure sand quite close to the sea and will put up with a lot of splashing, even by sea water.

SOIL PREPARATION

Remember that a hedge is going to be down for a number of years and so it is well worthwhile preparing the soil properly, forking the land over very shallowly, and adding bonemeal at 3–4 oz per square yard, and a good fish manure at a similar rate. If the land is very sandy it would be wise to add sedge peat or hop manure at $\frac{1}{2}$ lb per square yard as a top dressing. Remember to remove all the perennial weeds and their roots. If the soil is very wet it is worthwhile digging down 2 ft and burying some clinkers. bricks or other rubble down below to act as good drainage.

PLANTING

Mark out with a line the exact site where the hedge is going to be, and then dig out a trench in the prepared soil large enough to accommodate all the roots naturally. The distance apart that hedging plants will be put in will depend on the kinds to be planted: 15 ins apart is best for quick and myrobolan plum; 18 ins apart is the right distance for berberis, lonicera nidita, beech, hornbeam, holly, privet and escallonia; 2 ft apart must be allowed for veronicas, thuyas, cupressus, euonymus, tamarisk, cotoneasters and the larger barberries. A hedge that is to be planted near a fence or wall in order to clothe it should be put in at least 2 ft away.

In all cases buy young plants with good roots. Don't buy old hedging plants with few roots. The roots are more important than the tops. The only hedging plant perhaps that can be bought large is the Holly, which you can have as high as 5 ft.

PRUNING AND MAINTENANCE

Cut the hedges hard back for the first year or two to make them branch out well from the bottom. If you want a very thick hedge you can have two rows of bushes, arranged alternately. The result, however, is never so good as hard pruning plus patience, and a single row. Cut the hedges regularly as they grow, but do not cut evergreens after August or early September or the side shoots may die as a result of the frost. Do not cut them before they start to make growth in April. The larger leaved, shrubby hedges, such as laurel and holly, are best pruned back with a pair of secateurs, in May and again in August.

Don't forget to feed a hedge just as you would any other plant in the garden. If you do this you will get quicker and better growth. Apply a good fish manure at the rate of 1 oz per square yard in April and May, and again in June. In the autumn rake well underneath the hedge to remove dead leaves and any other rubbish that may have collected. Such material should be burned, since hedge bottoms are often the breeding ground for pests and diseases.

7 Roses

SOIL

It is really astonishing in how many different and varied soils roses seem to grow satisfactorily. The very light sands and sharp gravels do not suit them well, however, unless they are properly mulched with compost. It is difficult, also, to grow the best blooms on chalky soils.

Roses will grow quite well in boggy soils, provided they are properly drained. Perhaps the best soil, however, is a rich, heavy loam, which must be well drained and be well away from tall and overhanging trees.

If your soil is not ideal, you can improve it in various ways. Prepare the ground, for instance, by light forking, adding at the same time properly rotted powdery compost at the rate of one good barrowload to every 8 sq. ft, and during the final raking level give 4 oz of a good fish fertilizer and 4 oz of wood ashes per square yard. Lastly, just before the roses are ready to put in, hydrated lime can be applied on the surface if the ground is acid and has not been limed recently. A good dressing would be 6 oz to the square yard.

Sandy soils and gravels should have, in addition to the compost, a liberal dressing of sedge peat raked into the top. After the roses are in position in any soil the ground should be mulched with sedge peat 1 in. deep to hold moisture and prevent annual weeds from growing.

The roots of the roses, when planted, should never come into contact with manure; to prevent this, always give the compost as a top dressing.

MANURES

It is generally accepted that compost or sedge peat should be used liberally as a top dressing or mulch. A fish fertilizer is much recommended also; use up to 4 oz per square yard. Potash will be necessary, especially on lighter soils, and wood ashes can be used at 4–5 oz per square yard. These are particularly useful. Every year it is usual to give a light mulching of sedge peat, which acts not only as a humus provider, but is useful in dry years in preventing the moisture in the soil from evaporating.

PLANTING

Roses can be planted at any time from the third week in October until the middle of March. It will much depend on the soil, and when it can be prepared. The period before December is advisable. If the weather is bad, or if there are very heavy frosts, delay planting until March.

Do not plant on a wet day, when the soil is sticky. Even if the weather is good it is not a bad plan to have under cover

Rose planting: note the spread out roots. The branches will be pruned
a few weeks later

some fine soil with which to fill in part of the hole at planting time. This dry soil should be used for covering the roots, and the wetter soil can then be placed on top.

When the bushes arrive from the nursery, open the package and, unless the weather is frosty, heel the plants in immediately – that is to say, dig a hole and bury the roots temporarily. It is important that the roots do not get exposed to the wind or sun, which would dry them. If the ground is too hard for the heeling-in process, cover the roots with a damp sack and keep them under cover. Remove all the leaves and any seed pods on the branches and, before the bushes are actually put into the hole, prune the roots. The long ones may be trimmed back, and the damaged ones cut back to a healthy part, using a sharp knife.

When making the hole, see that it is large enough for the roots to be spread out evenly from the centre, and deep enough so that the base of the plant (where it was originally budded) is at least 1 in. below the level of the soil. Place the plant in the hole, separate out the roots and put them in their right position, and then fill in with some of the dry soil you have put by. Use small amounts of soil at a time. Get someone to hold the bush and to lift it up and down gently while you are putting the soil into position; in this way it will get all round the roots evenly. When 1 in. of soil has been added, tread down firmly, and every inch of soil added must be followed by firm treading with a heavy boot. Finally, rake over the surface of the ground so as to leave a little loose soil at the top.

If the planting is done early, very severe frosts that follow may sometimes damage the plants, and the thaw which follows may lift the bushes out of position. It may be worthwhile giving the newly planted roses some protection, and bracken or straw does this quite well. You can either just put bracken loosely around the plants or you can tie one of the bottle straw envelopes round the base. When the thaw sets in, be sure to go over the beds and tread round every plant. After treading, hoe the beds and rake the top of the soil.

Standard roses must be staked at planting. See that the stake comes right into the head, and then tie the rose securely at the top. Unless you do this, the roots never have a chance of growing, because they are being rocked about in the soil. The heads, also, may get damaged unless they are securely tied into position.

Normally the bushes will be planted 2 ft apart, but strong

growers will need 2½ ft. When planting a bed do not plant the outside rows any closer than 18 ins from the edge of the bed, though in the case of the dwarf polyantha types, 12 ins from the edge may do. It is becoming fashionable to plant roses much closer than this, as people seem to have a horror of seeing soil in between. If this is your choice, you can plant hybrid teas as close as 15 ins, and the strong growing varieties 18 ins apart.

Whatever you do, see that the roses are labelled directly after planting. Good, permanent labels are well worth having.

PRUNING

Most newcomers to gardening seem to regard rose pruning as something extremely difficult, and yet actually it is compatatively simple.

Roses are pruned every year in order that the bush may grow wider and the blooms may be larger and better. You must aim at producing fresh, healthy growths every year, and in doing so you will keep the bush really dwarf.

As a general guide, if a bush is growing vigorously you need not cut it hard, but if, on the other hand, it is not growing well, it needs to be cut very hard indeed. There seems to be a connection between the quality of the bloom and the strength of the growth that bears it. So if you cut hard, you get a strong growth and good blooms as well. There is something also in the place from which the growth emanates, and it seems that, provided of course you do not cut down below the budded part, the lower you cut, the stronger the resultant branch.

THE NEWLY PLANTED BUSH

This will not be pruned immediately after planting, but will be left until the normal time – either the end of March in the south or the first or second week in April in the north. The bush must be cut well back in the first year, to help it to establish itself and to get good branches. Each shoot then will be cut well down to within two or three good, plump, easily recognizable buds at the base. Cut to an outward-growing bud – this means make the cut at an angle of 45 degrees, with secateurs, just above a plump, outward-growing bud.

SUBSEQUENT PRUNING

After this, it is not necessary to be quite so severe. The general idea is to cut back to six good eyes (ie buds), being certain to keep the centre of the bush open. Remove all the weak shoots,

'Naughty Nancy', a creamy red rose, a Floribunda

and cut, say, one of the stronger shoots hard back to the base.

Do not be worried about the strong shoots which sometimes grow up from the variety itself, and learn to recognize these from the growths that come up from the roots, called suckers. These strong variety growths do help to maintain and prolong the life of the bush, and should not be pruned too hard in consequence.

RAMBLERS

Ramblers include wichurianas, climbing polyanthas and multifloras. These, when newly planted, should be pruned back to seven or eight eyes, and the weak growths cut out altogether. It is true that by pruning in this way you sacrifice bloom for the first season, but you will get good strong growths that will blossom profusely the following year.

In the following seasons prune back the growth immediately after flowering, making certain to cut out the shoots that have bloomed. The new growths made that season are then tied up in their place.

CLIMBING HYBRID TEAS

These must be pruned in quite a different manner from the ramblers. In the first place they are pruned at the end of March or at the beginning of April, and in the second place they must not be pruned too hard or else they lose their climbing habits and revert to the bush type. It is usual to cut back two or three of the strongest growths by one-third of their length, and to cut back the weak and the unripe shoots to four or six eyes. Once the trees are established you want to encourage lateral growths, as it is these that flower profusely. This is done by training the main shoots in a horizontal position, or, if you are growing them up posts, by winding them round like a screw thread. Whatever you do, do not tie them up vertically like ramblers.

STANDARDS

These trees may be pruned in the same way as bush plants, but it is usual to study the shape of the head very carefully when so doing.

WEEPING STANDARDS

Keep the shape of the head in perfect symmetry, remove the older shoots as necessary, and see that the branches are evenly placed. Always prune weeping standards hard the first March after planting.

A pink and salmon floribunda with H.T. like blooms
'Paddy McGredy'

FLORIBUNDAS

If you are using these for bedding, you can cut them quite hard every year. Normally all that is done is to cut away the old flower stems every March, and to thin out the old wood. This applies also to dwarf polyanthas.

GENERAL CULTIVATION

Keep the beds hoed throughout the summer unless you are adopting the sedge peat mulching system when there will be no hoeing to do, as there will be no annual weeds. The sedge peat covers the soil to a depth of 1 in. Even if the old-fashioned hoeing system is being adopted the bushes can be mulched before the hot weather sets in, and water can be given if the soil is too dry.

Whatever you do, never mulch roses with dung in the late autumn. This keeps the bed wet and cold. If some protection must be given, use sedge peat. Cut off all the blooms as soon as they start to fade. Never allow seed pods to form. If flowers are not wanted for decoration inside, do not ruin the bushes by leaving the flowers on the plant to seed. Cut roses with nice long stems during June and July – you can then ensure good blooms during September.

DISBUDDING

When growing varieties that produce good firm blooms, disbud them to leave only one flower bud to swell and develop at the end of a shoot. Do this disbudding early, and do not leave it until the colour is showing. The best time to do this work is when the buds are smaller than peas.

SUCKERING

Most roses are budded on to a type of briar root, and it is this briar that often tries to assert itself. It may suddenly send up a shoot from the roots, which can be distinguished from the cultivated variety by its wild look. If you are in doubt as to whether the shoot you are examining is a sucker or not, trace it down to the point from which it emanates. If this is below the point at which the rose bush was budded, it is obviously a wild briar, and should be cut out immediately to the base.

PESTS AND DISEASES

You must be on the look-out for greenfly all the time, and encourage the ladybirds which will eat the greenfly as well as

Cottage garden

Wall plants

Mixed hedge

their young. Rose trees that are not pruned hard enough, trees that are too near a shrubbery or in the shade or bigger trees, and trees near the house usually suffer far worse than those in open situations. Roses always do better when they are grown in an open place which gets all the sun and yet is not too windswept.

Keep an eye open for mildew and black spot – the latter is invariably controlled when the proper organic mulch is given (1 in. deep, as powdery compost or sedge peat). For a more detailed look at all these problems see my book on pests and diseases in this series.

VARIETIES

There are a very large number of varieties. I have made my own personal choice; for further information please consult my book *Basic Book of Rose Growing*.

HYBRID TEAS

Red

Alec's Red	Bright crimson. Bushy growth, large flowers.
Lucy Cramphorn	Geranium red. Large, well-formed flowers, spoil in rain.
Crimson Glory	Dark red. Free-flowering, medium to large blooms.
Etoile de Hollande	A bright, dark red. Large petals, foliage dark bronze-green.
Fragrant Cloud	Dusky scarlet, turns crimson, large, shapely flowers. Fragrant.
McGredy's	Long bud, strong growth. Foliage attractive dark green.
Ernest H. Morse	Bright ruby red. Large, well-formed flowers. Vigorous growth.
Orion	Light crimson. Free-flowering, bushy growth. Very healthy.
Pape Meilland	Very dark red. Substantial flowers. Glorious high-centred form.
Super Star	A lustrous, pure light vermilion. Medium-size flowers. Lovely form.

Blush Rose

Elizabeth Harkness	Off-white by creamy buff with flushes at centre, rose/amber. Large flowers, beautifully formed.

Lady Sylvia	Light pink. Free-flowering. Medium-size flower of neat form.
Madam Abel Chatenay	Rose-pink with silver reflex. Flowers freely. Good shape.
Madame Butterfly	Blush with touch of yellow. Regular form, medium-size flowers.
Pink Favourite	Bright, deep rose-pink. Large, well-formed flowers. Healthy.
Ophelia	Lightest blush, some gold at petal base. Regular form, free-flowering.
Wendy Cussons	Rose-red, opening to deep pink. Large flowers, well formed.

Orange and apricot

Apricot Silk	Deep orange with flushes of red. Large, well-formed flowers.
Emma Wright	Orange. Pointed and shapely bud. Dark green, glossy foliage. Ideal in habit of growth. Very free-flowering.
Chicago Peace	Pink with yellow reverse. Well-formed, large flowers. Bushy growth. Above average height.
Miss Ireland	Coral, shaded yellow, lighter reverse. Medium-size flowers. Well formed. Fairly free-flowering.
Mrs Sam McGredy	Scarlet coppery orange. Good-shaped flower. Bronze-green foliage. Spectacular and scented.
Piccadilly	Flame, scarlet and light yellow; well formed, moderately full with large flowers.
Whisky Mac	Light amber. Medium-size blooms, free-flowering, average height or less. Slight scent. Some liability to mildew.

Golden yellow

Grandpa Dickson	Light yellow, tending to greenish lemon early in blooming. Deeper yellow with red flushes later. High-centred form. Superb.
Grandmère Jenny	Light yellow, heavily veined and flushed deep pink. Free-flowering

	with slim blooms, opening large and perfect in form.
Isobel Harkness	Deep, bright yellow. Tight buds open to loose flowers of medium size. Free-flowering. Growth bushy and upright.
Peace	Light yellow, flushed pink. Large flowers, superb in form. Exhibition quality. Slight scent.
Spek's Yellow	Bright golden-yellow. Bloom large. Foliage dark green, glossy, stout and large. Growth bushy and compact.
Sutter's Gold	Clear yellow, flushed pink. Flowers of medium size. Beautifully formed, not full. Free-flowering. Sweet scent.

White

Frau Karl Druschki	A good grower. Must be disbudded. Foliage bright and glossy.
Marcia Stanhope	Perfectly shaped. Lemon tinge at centre. Tremendous blooms. Foliage pale green. Fragrance reminiscent of verbena.
Pascali	Medium-sized flowers, well formed. Vigorous growth. Free-flowering.
Virgo	Flowers of medium size, attractive form. Free-flowering. Moderate growth. Slightly scented. May be subject to mildew.

Salmon

Harlow	Salmon pink. Free-flowering, well-formed flowers. Slight scent.
My Choice	Bicolour, pink with light yellow reverse. Large, well-formed flowers.
Shot Silk	Rosy carmine, flushed salmon. Well-formed, medium-size flowers.
Violinista Costa	Salmon pink, flushed red. Medium-size flowers, open quickly.

Various shades

| Blue Moon | Light lilac. Well-formed, large flowers with high centres. Free-flowering and bushy in growth. Extremely fragrant. |

Portadown Fragrance | An orange-salmon pink, shaded with orange scarlet. Bears large flowers on long stems. Foliage bronze-green. One of the most deliciously scented roses.

FLORIBUNDAS

Red

Dr Barnardo | Deep crimson. Good bud form opening to double flowers. Some open split but are a spectacular crimson. Strong growth.

Frensham | Bright crimson. Attractive bud form opens to semi-double. Free-flowering. Shiny, bright green leaves. Liable to mildew.

Dorothy Wheatcroft | Scarlet. Semi-double flowers. Vigorous growth but rather shrubby. Above average height. Healthy.

Evelyn Fison | Vivid scarlet. Large-headed, semi-double flowers. Free-flowering, average height, bushy growth. Usually healthy but can mildew.

Glengarry | Vivid vermilion red. Well-formed flowers with high centres. Bushy growth, free-flowering. Usually healthy. Slightly scented.

Lively Lady | Vermilion, slight rosiness. Beautifully formed flowers. Upright, bushy growth. Average height. Slightly scented. Healthy.

Lilli Marlene | Deep, bright crimson. Compact, free-flowering. Bushy growth. Average height. Usually healthy but can mildew. Semi-double blooms.

Red Dandy | Bright crimson. Beautiful, full flowers, not crowded. Vigorous, free-flowering growth. Slightly scented. Usually healthy.

Orangeade | Bright vermilion red. Virtually single flowers showing centres. Free-flowering. Vigorous growth. Average height, bushy. Healthy.

Orange Sensation	Bright vermilion. Double flowers on small side, very pretty form. Bushy, free-flowering growth. Pleasant scent.
Scarlet Queen Elizabeth	Bright, deep scarlet. Rounded centre, semi-double blooms. Above-average height, strong and bushy. Usually healthy.

Pink

Dearest	Rose pink, tinged with salmon. Buds open to rather full flowers that dislike rain. Usually healthy. Pleasantly scented.
Chanelle	Near white with pink flush. Free-flowering and bushy in growth. Slightly scented and average in height. Well-formed, large heads.
Fairy Dancers	Creamy buff and light rose. Unusual shade. Beautifully formed flowers with neat centres. Free-flowering, low growth.
Paddy McGredy	Deep pink, sometimes carmine. Large, well-formed flowers. Close together. Bushy, compact and free-flowering. Slightly perfumed.
Pink Parfait	Light rose-pink, sometimes veined a deeper pink or suffused creamy yellow. Flowers with exquisite centres. Usually healthy.
Queen Elizabeth	Clear pink. Large, well-formed blooms. Good for cutting. Growth strong, easily reaching twice average height. Upright bush.
Violet Carson	Light pink with deeper flush. Beautifully formed double flowers with large heads. Vigorous growth. Free-flowering.

Salmon

Elizabeth of Glamis	Light salmon. Well-formed flowers. Growth bushy and free-flowering. Average height or less. Usually healthy.
Margo Koster	Salmon with some reversion to red.

| | Bowl-like blooms, small. Short growth and bushy. Free-flowering. Usually healthy. Scented. |
| Mrs Richards | Rosey salmon. Single blooms with lighter centres. Close together with large heads. Bushy, free-flowering. Lovely foliage. |

Orange and flame

Golden Slippers	Bicolour, orange red with yellow reverse. Attractive buds.
Masquerade	Yellow, turning pink and red. Well-formed buds give semi-double blooms. Bushy growth. Free-flowering and upright. Slight scent.
Pineapple Poll	Yellow, flushed orange to orange-red. Small, double flowers. Very neat. Below-average height. Healthy appearance. Fruity scent.
Woburn Abbey	Orange, made by orange, red and yellow. Attractive buds open to semi-double flowers borne on large heads. Slightly perfumed.

Yellow

Allgold	Golden yellow. Semi-double, well-formed blooms. Free-flowering and compact in growth. Slight scent. Below-average height.
Golden Jewel	Clear yellow. Many-petalled, double flowers. Short growth, free-flowering. Usually healthy. Slightly perfumed.
Honeymoon	Bright yellow turning to cream. Well-formed double flowers. Upright, free-flowering growth. Above-average height. Usually healthy.
Yellow Cushion	Clear yellow turning to cream. Free-flowering and with many petals. Average height or less. Slightly scented and usually healthy.

Lilac

| Escapade | Light rosy magenta with white centre. Virtually single large-headed |

| | blooms. Bushy, free-flowering growth. Healthy usually. Scented. |
| News | Bright purplish magenta. Free-flowering semi-double flowers. Bushy, slightly scented and of average height. |

White

| Iceberg | White but sometimes flushed with pink. Neatly formed semi-double heads. Stand bad weather well. Free-flowering and bushy in growth. |

CLIMBING ROSES

The following are the best climbers I have grown.

Red

Climbing Ena Harkness	Bright velvety crimson. Exquisite and regular in form. Free-flowering for about 4 weeks in season. Some later blooms.
Climbing Etoile de Hollande	Dark red. Buds open loosely; free-flowering for about 4 weeks in summer. Strong growth. Usually healthy.
Parkdirektor Riggers	Bright scarlet. Semi-double blooms, small and close together. Some autumn bloom. Average growth. Excellent foliage.
Paul's Scarlet Climber	Bright scarlet. Semi-double, small flowers. Free-flowering for about 6 weeks in summer. Vigorous growth. Average height. Usually healthy but some mildew.

Pink and salmon

| Climbing Lady Sylvia | Light pink. Neat form. Medium-size blooms of clean appearance. Very vigorous, tall growth. Sweetly scented. |
| Climbing Mrs Sam McGredy | Coppery pink, flushed red to pink. Free-flowering with some autumn bloom. Vigorous growth, handsome foliage. Scented. May black spot. |

Climbing Shot Silk	Rosy carmine flushed salmon. Well-formed flowers of medium size. Free-flowering in summer. Vigorous growth. Sweet scent.
Francis Juranville	Rose pink. Attractive form with small semi-double blooms. Excellent foliage and free-flowering in summer. Healthy. Scented.
Pink Perpetué	Deep pink. Double blooms of medium size. Free-flowering summer and autumn. Restrained height, good growth. Slightly scented.
Zephirine Drouhin	Deep pink. Medium-size flowers, often quartered. Attractive and free-flowering in summer. Good also in autumn. Sweet perfume.

Yellow

Climbing Sutter's Gold	Clear yellow, flushed pink. Beautifully formed medium-size flowers. Not full. Free-flowering in summer and later.
Emily Gray	Rich yellow. Double, well-formed flowers, small, open loosely. Free-flowering in summer. Strong. Usually healthy but can mildew.
Golden Showers	Bright yellow, turns to pale yellow. Long, well-formed buds open semi-double to show stamens. Restrained grower, rather bushy.

White

White Cockade	Well-formed flowers, double and of medium size. Free-flowering summer and autumn. Usually healthy and strong in growth. Scented.
Kiftsgate	Small, single blooms on large heads. Free-flowering in early summer. Extremely vigorous in growth. Usually healthy. Sweetly perfumed.

Cream

Alberic Barbier	Semi-double. Well-formed buds. Free-flowering in summer for 5

New Dawn

weeks, scattered bloom in autumn.
Strong grower. Usually healthy.
Soft pearl. Well-formed, small
blooms with high centres. Extremely
free-flowering. Strong growth but
not tall. Usually healthy. Scented.

Rose—'Madame Alfred Carrière'

8 The rock garden

Most people seem to want to have a rock garden of some sort, even if it is quite small. If you are keen on making a large rock garden read *Basic Book of Rock Gardens and Pools*.

THE SITE

A great deal depends on the position and shape of the ground, but a sunny site should be chosen, as nearly all alpine plants are used to unrestricted light. Secondly, the rock garden should be sited where it can be a separate feature. Even a belt of shrubs, planted on purpose, is a better division than no separation at all.

Never plan a rock garden near elms or sycamores or, in fact, near any large trees, as they send out their roots tremendous distances and rob the rock plants of food and moisture.

If the site chosen has a slight slope, so much the better, as it is much easier to place the rocks naturally and to produce pleasing effects. If the ground is not variable in contour, then an attempt must be made to break up the outline by forming mounds of earth and by putting the stone into suitable positions. Another thing that can be done is to position the path below the natural level of the soil, so that you have to look up to the garden.

It is not advisable to make a rock garden in a low-lying place, which will tend to be damp, and, unless drained very thoroughly, will give you a lot of trouble.

In a small garden do not attempt anything too elaborate. See that your rocks look natural by all means, and try to give height by planting an evergreen shrub or two. In the same way it is better to have the highest point at one end and a point not quite so high at the other. The intervening space can be naturally undulating, but not too symmetrical.

There should be no difficulty in the choice or number of plants, as most of the finest specimens grow no larger than an area which can be covered with a 3-in. flower pot even when fully grown. So there is no reason why a large number of different types and varieties should not be grown in even the smallest rock garden. Choose plants of a neat-growing habit, and you can have a rock garden in miniature. On a small rockery the trees and shrubs that are used must be small themselves, or the whole of the proportion is lost.

The large rock garden should be planned in a way that resembles nature at her best. The outcropping on the Derbyshire hills and moors and in the gorges of Somerset will show you how the rocks ought to be placed in position. A winding path can traverse the garden, while it goes up the gorge and down into the little valley. Bold masses here and there can swell out, while secondary valleys can be arranged as you think fit.

During all this, take care that there are pockets and crevices facing in all directions, so that you can grow plants that like sun, shade, and so on. Consider having steps of rough-hewn stone or a path of crazy paving, in the crevices of which certain plants will grow.

SUITABLE ROCK MATERIALS

It is not everyone who can afford to buy rock brought from long distances. Beautiful weathered limestone can be obtained from Derbyshire and other counties of the northern midlands. I know of some lovely rock gardens made of Cotswold stone. Those who live in Kent may like Kentish rag, while sandstones from Surrey and Sussex are much admired. Granite is sometimes used, though on the whole the harder stones of this character do not absorb moisture, and so do not encourage plants to cling to them.

Fairly 'soft' stone on the whole is advisable, but not so soft that it is easily damaged and flakes in frosty weather. Use natural stone if possible in every case. Do not use artificial or reconstituted stone if you can avoid it. In the same way, concrete and brick-bats are neither natural nor beautiful.

The stones should be, if possible, at least 2 ft in length, and of about the same breadth. Even larger stones can be used in more extensive rock gardens.

SOIL

You will probably have to use the soil already in your garden as a basis for pockets and for the general mass used in making up mounds and undulations. But it is well worth importing or making up special pockets for plants that need specific types of soil. It may be that your soil is too heavy or too damp.

Perhaps it contains too little 'fibre' and needs organic material added to it. Study the plants you are going to grow. Read about them, and find out their habits. In this way you will be able to produce the right mixture for individual plants.

The pockets may contain only 18 ins of soil, but below there will be a good root run. Quite a good general mixture would be eight parts of ordinary garden soil, mixed with half a part of coarse sand and half a part of rock chippings. Add sedge peat if the soil is of a heavy, clayey character. Just before planting, other materials may have to be incorporated – more peat for some plants and bushes, more sand for others.

Do not forget that some alpines like a good deal of crushed limestone or granite. The granite will suit those that dislike lime in any form. Many of the smaller androsaces like more than a quarter of the compost to consist of grit, while the strong saxifrages will do quite well in ordinary loam. Gentians like peat, and so do primulas and lithospermums.

BUILDING THE ROCK GARDEN

Always start at the lowest point by bedding the base rocks in the ground. At least two-thirds of the rock should be buried to make it look like a natural outcrop, and they should incline towards the main body of soil in which they rest. This slight tilting backwards helps to guide the rain down to the roots of the plants. As the other rocks are placed in position they may have a tilt either to the right or to the left. Whatever tilt is given to the lower stones, the higher ones should follow the same sequence – at any rate for a good distance.

As the stones are put into position, suitable soil may be placed behind them and rammed lightly to keep them in position. Do not forget the pockets, which may be as large as 3 ft square even if these large ones have smaller rocks peeping through. As I have said before, do make it look natural, and for this reason do not build pinnacle-like effects. There is no reason why grass should not form part of your rock garden scheme – in fact, stones outcropping from grass look both natural and fascinating.

Even in a small rock garden see that certain stones have a flat surface, to act as stepping stones for getting about from place to place.

As a last word of warning, whatever you do do not stick your stones into the ground so that they look like almonds in a trifle.

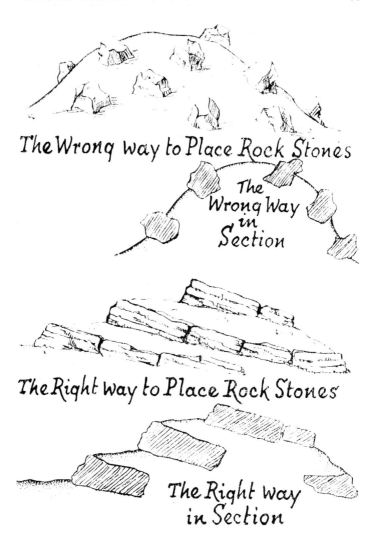

Building the rock garden

PLANTING

Once the rock garden is made, most people want to see it furnished and carpeted at the earliest possible moment. There are several plants that will do this quickly, but because they are strong growing they are apt to smother the weaker and choicer plants. Be sure not to overdo the strong growers and, once you have planted them, see that you cut them back and keep them within bounds. The following are quick-growing, and should be watched carefully: iberis, aubretia, cerastium, arabis and alyssum saxatile.

Planting can be done at any time in autumn and spring, provided the ground is fit to work. As the rock garden is often at its best in late spring, autumn planting is on the whole preferable.

The next point to consider is the likes and dislikes of the plants you are going to grow. Many of the primulas like moisture – for example, primula bulleyana – and so should be planted in the lower positions, and near water if you have a small pool. The sempervivums and sedums would soon rot away if they were planted in such a position. The members of the dianthus family like sun, while the oxalis like shade.

Plant firmly. Make a hole with a trowel, put the plant in position so that it is at the right level, and make the soil all round it very firm. See that there is no hollow beneath it, and press down all round the base of the roots. There is a great danger, when planting clefts of rocks, of loose soil at the base. It is better to ram the soil into position first of all, making certain that it is sufficiently open by putting some gritty material in with the compost. Do not plant so deeply as to bury the plants, but see that they are not out of the soil and left high and dry.

After planting, label the groups.

GENERAL CULTIVATION

During the year weed regularly. This usually means going over the garden about once a fortnight, stirring the soil with a little hand fork, and removing the weeds by hand. This kind of regular attention, which need only take half an hour or so in small gardens, saves hours of work later on.

As soon as the groups of plants have flowered, all the dead flowers and stems should be cut off. The stronger growing types should be cut back to prevent them spoiling other plants – and, in fact, spoiling themselves.

Early in February the aubretias and mossy saxifrages which may seem nearly dead should have the straggling growths removed from the brown patches. A little sifted soil may then be given as a top dressing, forked in lightly here and there.

Many of the early-flowering types have their blooms damaged by birds when they are in the bud stage, and these will need protection with little twiggy pieces of wood – push them in around the plants, with strands of black cotton stretched in between them.

Some plants are apt to die during the winter, not so much because of the frost, but because of the damp. They should be covered with a small piece of glass before the winter starts.

A sheet of glass supported on wire stays

Winter protection for a tender rock plant

Many of the androsaces, and the less hardy sempervivums, have to be treated in this way.

CONIFERS
If you want a Lilliputian effect in your rock garden, nothing helps more than planting miniature conifers that are in themselves perfect in shape and yet never grow to any size.

The following are suitable varieties:

Cupressus obtusavvar caespitosa	Produce moss-like dense tuffets. Rounded growth.
Cupressus plumosa aurea compacta	Golden. Miniature cone-shaped.
Picea albertiana conica	Pyramidal in shape. Grows very slowly. Likes moist soil and a sheltered position.
Taxus baccata pygmaea	Very dwarf. Beautiful green.
Taxus compacta	Slow-growing and compact.
Thuya plicata aurea Rogersii	Pyramidal form. Gold and bronze foliage.
Ulex nanus	Dwarf gorse, flowers September.

BULBS
Many of the dwarfer-growing bulbous plants are very suitable for the rock garden. They will grow in light soil, and the depth

of planting varies according to the size of the bulb. Types and varieties can be obtained which flower at different periods of the year.

Here are a few examples:

SPRING-FLOWERING BULBS

Allium in variety; anemone in variety; chionodoxa and crocus, several species; fritillaria in variety; iris, reticulata, histrioides, and warleyensis; muscari ; scilla in variety; many dwarf tulips.

SUMMER-FLOWERING BULBS

Allium pulchellum; oxalis floribunda; tritonia crocata.

AUTUMN-FLOWERING BULBS

Crocus, various varieties; cyclamen africanum; cyclamen europaeum, c. neapolitanum; scilla autumnalis.

WINTER-FLOWERING BULBS

Anemone, various varieties; crocus, various varieties; galanthus in variety; iris alata, i. persica, i. reticulata, and i. stylosa.

LIST OF ROCK PLANTS PARTIAL TO PARTICULAR PLACES OR CONDITIONS

SHADE-LOVING PLANTS

Androsace oliosa; arenaria balearica; cyanthus lobatus; primulas in variety; ramondia; ferns and aconites.

PLANTS FOR HALF-SHADE

Androsace arachnoida; aquilegia caerulea; aster alpinus; campanula pulla; epigaea repens; erodium chamaedryoides; mertensia in variety; primulas in variety; the mossy saxifrages; viola pedata.

PLANTS THAT LOVE MOISTURE

Mimulus; lysimachia; parnassia; trillium.

PLANTS DISLIKING DAMP

(In winter, these should always be covered with a piece of glass a few inches above them.)

Androsace; artemisia lanata; asperula suberosa; campanula hirsuta; the tufted dianthus; helichyrsum frigidum; hypericum coris and tomentosum; lychnis alpina; papaver alpinum.

PLANTS FOR WALLS

Saponaria ocymoides; alyssum saxatile; aethionema warley

rose; dianthus caesiùs; iberis snowflake; campanula portensch-
lagiana; corydalis lutea; linaria; erinus; aubretias.

CRAZY-PAVING PLANTS

Achillea tomentosa; alyssum montanum; antennaria tomentosa; dianthus deltoides; erinus alpinus; mentha requieni;
thymus lanuginosus, t. serpyllum and t. Annie Hall; sedum
lydium; cotula squalida.

9 Lawns

There are two ways of making a lawn – one by seeding, and the other by turfing.

SOIL PREPARATION

Lawns seem to grow best on a medium loam, and so you should aim at producing a soil as near to this character as possible. With heavy clay soils you will need to add sand, powdery, dark brown compost or even finely ground sedge peat. With sandy soils it is a help to fork in some moisture-holding material, like coarse sedge peat, to prevent the soil drying out too much during the summer.

There is no need to dig deeply, especially if the soil is already of the right character. Just aim at making the top 1–2 ins in a nice friable condition. If you are forking in organic matter like compost, do this to a depth of 4 ins. Be sure the land is well drained. It is most annoying, especially if you want to use the lawn for games, to find that it is impossible to play on it because it is sodden after rain.

You will probably need to level the ground, and you must take care not to bring subsoil to the surface. I have known gardens where, to get a level surface, the top soil from one end of the proposed lawn had been wheeled to the other end. The result, of course, is a double depth of good soil on one side, and only subsoil left at the other. Though it seems a good deal of extra work, the only thing to do is to take away the top soil and place it in a heap nearby. The subsoil is then dug up and put in its new position, and the top soil from the heap is replaced. In this way you get the level you require – and the whole surface is covered with good soil.

Often, with new houses, the builder has put a good deal of subsoil dug up when preparing foundations, all over the soil you have to use. Stones, lime and other kinds of rubbish are often included, too. This unwanted material must be removed.

Having got your levels right, the next thing to do is to decide whether the land is really clean enough to sow the seed or not. If you are satisfied that you are not going to get a heavy crop of weeds, you can sow immediately, but, if not, you should fallow the land to eradicate weeds.

SEED SOWING

Seed can be sown in either spring or autumn. My experience in the north midlands tells me that spring is probably better there, while in the south-east autumn sowing is usually preferable. The severe winters in the north-west, and the very heavy winter rains, never give the young grasses much chance. The south-east often gets a dry May and June, so that spring sowing often means poor germination and poor growth.

If sowing is done in spring the land should be forked in the autumn, compost incorporated (rotted leaf mould, sand, or whatever you are going to use), and the land left fairly rough. The land should be forked over 2–3 ins deep in spring, and allowed to lie bare for a period of three weeks to a month. During this time weeds will, of course, grow, and so, before sowing the seed, they should be hoed down and raked off. Fallowing is a good plan – leave the land bare all the first summer, so you can hoe continuously and eradicate all the weeds. Do not miss the opportunity of getting rid of both annual and perennial weeds at the start. I have seen many lawns ruined through careless preparation.

The kind of lawn you should aim for is one that consists of fine grasses and nothing else. The lawns that are full of clover and moss, or spoiled by daisies and plantains, are not worth having. Lawns will do well in all kinds of places, and under all kinds of conditions, if you lay them properly at the start.

If your land is stony, you may feel that you have to remove every stone before you start. Stones do no harm unless there is a very large number of them. If you bury large numbers of them when digging they will help with drainage.

Do not attempt to sow the seed until the surface has been raked down into a very fine condition. You want to get the land firm, and so you must roll it when the surface is dry. Alternate rolling and raking will enable you to do the final levelling. Then, just before you are ready to sow, roll again, and rake to produce a fine, loose, surface seed.

THE SEED

Buying good seed, of the right varieties, is very important. Do not just buy 'lawn seed' – lawn grasses have names just like other seeds. Many of the cheaper lawn seed mixtures contain a good deal of rye grass, and this never makes a perfect sward. Your lawn will be down for years, and if you can get it right at the start by using the right seed, you will never regret it.

But do not go from one extreme to another. It is not necessary to have a very complicated mixture. It is possible to produce a lawn by sowing one kind of seed only, and if you want to do this, use agrostis tenuis (commonly known as brown top bent). This is a poor starter, and often disappointing in the early stages; it is more suitable for heavier and medium soils than for light sands.

A very simple mixture, which has done well in many gardens, consists of

25 per cent agrostis tenuis

75 per cent Chewing's fescue

Increase the proportion of fescue and reduce the amount of agrostis if the soil be light.

Another popular mixture, which some people think is an improvement, is

5 parts Chewing's fescue

2 parts creeping red fescue

3 parts New Zealand bent

The disadvantage of the agrostis family is that the lawn may look 'benty' during a dry summer – the lawn looks brown, and seems covered with very fine strings.

A mixture which omits the bents is

25 per cent fine-leaved sheep's fescue

50 per cent Chewing's fescue

25 per cent sea-washed fescue

As a general rule people prefer to use the agrostis mixture, as it makes a lawn more quickly, and smothers out weeds more effectively.

Get a guarantee that the seed mixture is not weedy. It is most disheartening, having cleaned the land, to find you have inadvertently sown weeds again. Conversely it is pointless to sow seed of high purity on unclean land.

THE PROCESS OF SOWING

Sow evenly – this is really very important. Divide the seed into equal lots, and see that the right amount of seed covers the exact amount of ground. Sowing is made easier if the seed is mixed with a larger bulk of sand or sifted soil. Some people mark off the whole lawn into square-yard plots, by strings stretched from one end of the plot to the other, a yard apart, both down and across.

Sow on a still, dry day, when the surface is in a good friable condition. This may be any time from the middle of March to the end of April. After the even distribution of seed, rake the land over lightly. It is possible to sift some light soil over as a top dressing, first of all. When adding soil to cover seeds, take care, as very little is required. Anyway, the final operation will be a light rolling. This must only be done when the surface is dry.

AMOUNT OF SEED

Some gardeners advise $1\frac{1}{2}$ oz of seed to a square yard, and this is not far wrong when using the last two formulae mentioned. When an agrostis mixture is used alone, such as the agrostis tenuis, 5 'b of seed is sufficient for 100 sq. yds (1 oz to the square yard).

BIRDS

Birds can swoop down onto newly sown land and gobble up all the seeds. It does not matter if they only eat a few, but they can easily overdo it! You can cover the lawn with fruit tree netting, strung up on bamboos, or thread black cotton from twiggy sticks in a criss-cross manner, all over the surface. Products like. Morkit can be poured onto the seeds before they are sown, and this prevents them from being eaten. Some suppliers sell ready-treated seed.

TIME TO CUT

Do not be in too great a hurry to mow a newly laid lawn, since you may drag the young grasses up by the roots. In the same way it is inadvisable to walk all over the lawn when the young grass is growing. Wait until it is at least 2 ins high and then scythe it.

It is often difficult to scythe lawns in a small garden, and the alternative is to set the blades of your mower high and run it over the lawn once. If you can roll it a few days beforehand, so much the better. Even the next four or five cuts should be made with the blades in this position; then you can lower them and cut the lawn quite short.

I know small garden owners who have been patient enough to go over their new lawns with a pair of shears in the early stages, and this is indeed a good plan, though rather tiring.

Look out for weeds the whole time, and pull them out immediately they are seen. It is not a good plan to put on artificial
manures at this early stage. On lighter soils a top dressing may
be given with some finely ground peat, which not only helps
rooting but acts as a moisture-holder. New Zealand brown-top
sometimes damps off in the seedling stage, and requires quick-
acting nitrogen to help it through.

LAYING A LAWN WITH TURF

This is a far more expensive method, and, unless good turves
are obtained, free from weeds, it is not advised. It has the
advantage of ensuring that a good lawn is created far more
quickly, but needs far more expertise in the laying.

The turves usually arrive rolled up in lengths 3 ft long, 1 ft
broad, and $1\frac{1}{2}$ ins thick. It is best to lay them down in January,
as the turves will not knit with the soil underneath if the
weather is dry afterwards. But this does not mean that you
should lay them down during a wet period.

Put the turf down directly it arrives (it should not be stacked
for days – a lot of damage is done like this), if the weather is
suitable, on the prepared level soil. The preparation is exactly
the same as for sowing seed. Once the turves have been laid
down, beat them into position, one area at a time, with a turf
beater. Never over-beat – get the soil level first. When the
whole area has been covered, pass a heavy roller over to
consolidate it. If there are any spaces between the sods, and
these should be very small, fill them in with equal parts of fine
leaf mould and sand. Then roll the whole lawn over again.

LOOKING AFTER LAWNS

Having made your lawn, you will want to look after it with
care. It will need (1) regular cutting, (2) rolling, (3) feeding,
(4) spiking, (5) raking, (6) elimination of excess worms, (7)
control of pests and diseases.

REGULAR CUTTING

Whatever you do, never let a lawn go to seed. Cut it at least
once a week as soon as the warm weather starts in the spring,
and in the full flush of the summer, after a feed and after rain,
it may be necessary to cut twice a week. When the grass is
established, the knives can be set fairly low and the grass cut,
say, $\frac{3}{4}$ in. from the soil. If the weather becomes dry, you can

leave off the grass box and let the cut grass lie on the lawn to act as a mulch. Do not cut during frosty weather, but if the winter is mild you may have to start cutting early in March.

ROLLING

Much of the rolling will be done in winter when the soil is sufficiently moist. Rolling helps to level a lawn and to compact it. When used in the spring, a roller encourages the young grass to grow thickly. Never roll a lawn when it is covered with worm casts. Either brush them off or apply worm treatment before you start rolling.

A certain amount of rolling can be done in spring and summer, but it is not much use running a roller over dry ground.

With lawns on heavy soils be careful not to over-roll when the ground is sodden. It is better to wait until spring.

Regular rolling, backwards and forwards in long straight lines, is better than unmethodical meanderings.

FEEDING

The experiments that have been carried out at the Board of Greenkeeping Research Station in Yorkshire show that to produce the perfect sward, acidity is necessary. It is undoubtedly an advantage to have the surface layer of soil in a lawn acid. This seems to prevent the invasion of both worms and weeds. If you find it in an old lawn, preserve it at all costs. If the condition is absent, you can induce it by using powdered peat, sterilized compost and sharp sand. For this reason lime should be withheld. Don't be tempted to try to induce soil acidity by adding heavy dressings of fish manure. This must be regarded first and foremost as an organic fertilizer, and secondly, as a weed discourager.

The use of a liquid hormone like Verdone gives better weed control than chemical weedkillers. There is no need to use chemicals if all the weeds and mosses have already been eradicated by hormones and mercury. The only way, in fact, to control moss – apart from spiking to ensure good drainage – is to use some form of mercury, such as Calomel Dust at, say, 3–4 oz to the square yard.

Fish manure should be applied at the rate of 2 oz per square yard. The first application should be put on at Easter, and another similar dressing about six weeks later. Keep this fertilizer perfectly dry before it is applied, and crush up finely any lumps present. It is essential to apply this mixture evenly. Two methods can be recommended for applying fish manure. The first one is to throw the fertilizer well up into the air and allow it to fall down evenly as a powder, but there is a risk of having some parts untreated and others over-treated and scorched. The second method is to use a fertilizer distributor which can be bought at any garden shop. If you use the first method, to minimize the risk of scorching reduce the quantity to 1 oz per square yard, but increase the number of applications.

In addition to the fish fertilizer, it may be necessary in summer to give a top dressing of finely ground sedge peat, which not only improves the physical condition of the lawn but gives nitrogen at the same time.

SPIKING

A certain number of worms in a lawn are of value, as they tend to aerate it, and the worm casts they throw up provide a simple top dressing. Acid lawns never encourage worms, and so artificial spiking may have to be carried out. Use a spiked roller for large lawns; on a small lawn a long, fine-tined fork is adequate; push it in as deeply as possible all over the lawn every three years.

RAKING

When the lawn is composed largely of stoloniferous grasses (creeping bents), raking is particularly important and should be done before Easter. Try and start about the beginning of March – in the south, at any rate. Raking not only disturbs the dead stolons, but removes unwanted mosses.

ELIMINATION OF EXCESS WORMS

In the spring, if you find an overabundance of worm casts, use mowrah meal at 8 oz to the square yard. If this is done just before rain, you will have no further problems; in dry weather the mowrah meal will have to be watered in. The worms will rise to the surface in their thousands, and can be swept off.

CONTROL OF PESTS AND DISEASES

Lawns are often troubled by leather-jackets, the grub of the crane-fly, known to most of us as daddy-long-legs. This pest is particularly bad in the south of Britain and on sandy soils. The turf will be found dying in irregular patches, because the roots of the grasses have been eaten away. If the turf is lifted in these places, a tough-skinned grub will be found, about $1-1\frac{1}{2}$ ins long when fully grown, and of an earthy colour. There is no known way of keeping the female fly from laying her eggs in the lawn, but the grub may be exterminated by watering with a 64 per cent emulsion of orthodichloroben-zene; $\frac{1}{8}$ pint of this should be added to 7 gallons of water, which is sufficient for 200 sq. yds of lawn.

The disease which does most damage on lawns is fusarium patch caused by fusarium nivale. A small patch appears on the lawn about the size of a penny, and if examined carefully is found to consist of dying or dead bleached grass. The trouble can spread to form larger patches, about the shape of a Rugby football. To make certain that this is the cause of the trouble, cover the patch with a bottomless seed box, and place a piece of glass on the top. If in a day or so a pink or white growth appears, this indicates fusarium trouble. These patches must be removed bodily and burnt.

IMPROVING A NEGLECTED LAWN

In the case of a lawn which has been badly neglected for years, it may be necessary to treat the largest weeds with Selex, which can be bought in an aerosol. But it is no use removing large weeds without replacing them with something else. Fill the hole in with a light sedge peat compost, and then sow suitable lawn seed on the surface.

If moss is a bad problem and, after raking, the lawn looks very bare, it would be a good thing for the whole lawn to be top-dressed with a light soil mixed with sedge peat on a 50/50 basis, into which lawn seed has been mixed beforehand.

Apart from these two special operations, the usual applica-tions of fish manure must be put on at regular intervals. It is surprising how these applications, plus regular rolling and mowing, will improve the lawn out of all recognition in a very short time.

LIME

Lime is dangerous to use, as it causes weediness and suscepti-bility to disease. In dry years, however, limed lawns often remain green much longer. Don't be tempted to put lime on more often than every five years at the most, and then only in the autumn.

10 Vegetables – rotation of crops

The vegetable garden should be planned just like any other part of the garden. It should have enough paths in it so that manure etc. can be wheeled about in barrows, and so that cabbage stalks and other organic matter can be taken away to the compost heap. In the average small garden one well-placed path would be sufficient.

Whatever the size of the vegetable garden some system for the rotation of crops should be thought out. Some people, of course, do not want to grow all kinds of vegetables, but want to restrict the number to two or three. If so, the rotational scheme will be a very simple one. The aim is that the ground should be fully occupied for most of the year, and that no part of the garden is wasted. In a garden of this kind, the crops that are grown can be divided into three groups.

PERMANENT CROPS
Common examples are herbs, rhubarb, seakale, asparagus and globe artichokes, spinach beet and perpetual spinach.

CATCH CROPS
These are crops that only occupy the ground for a short space of time and do not form part of the rotational scheme. For instance, you can grow shallots along the ridges of celery trenches; radishes can be sown in between rows of peas when these are first put in. It is also possible to grow a catch crop during the period between harvesting one crop and sowing another. After an early crop of peas, which come off, say, at the end of July, you may not want to use the ground again until August or early September for autumn-sown onions. You have therefore got a month or two in which to produce a quick-growing catch crop.

Common catch crops are mustard and cress, radishes, French beans, early turnips, stump-rooted carrots and dwarf peas.

ANNUAL CROPS
Most vegetables fall into this category. Some crops take less than twelve months to mature, while others take the whole of or more than this period.

DOUBLE CROPPING OR INTER CROPPING
Keen gardeners can often save a week or two by planting or sowing one crop in between the rows of another before the original one is harvested. Some people plant Brussels sprouts or savoys between rows of early potatoes, but this is not a good plan as the brassicas always suffer. You can plant marrows in between rows of early peas, as the marrows like the shade of the peas in the early stages, and then, when the peas come out, the marrows get all the sun they want. Leeks can be planted in between peas in the same way. French beans may be sown in between rows of cabbages and, as the French beans start to require more room, the cabbages can be cut and used. Keen cultivators will be able to work out other and perhaps better schemes for saving time and space. Be careful not to overdo the idea, or neither crop will benefit. Some crops, however, actually prefer to grow near others, for instance, tomatoes do well when trained up sweet corn. Lettuces do well in between peas.

MANURIAL CROPPING
As manures play such an important part in arranging the rotation, it is as well to mention one or two useful points. The root crops – beet, carrots, parsnips etc. – will not grow to advantage in ground that has been freshly manured, as this causes them to fork and makes the roots useless. The cabbage family likes well-manured land, and needs a good dressing of nitrogen. Peas and beans, because of the nodular growths on their roots, can extract nitrogen out of the air, and so after they have cropped, if the roots are left behind, nitrogen is left also.

Potatoes, because of their particular method of growth, and because of the way they are cultivated, act as a good 'cleaning crop'. Potatoes are well manured, and so leave the soil in a high state of fertility. On the other hand, it is not usual to lime potatoes, and so the land may be slightly acid. Cabbages and peas like lime. Root crops like plenty of phosphates, while peas and beans like potash.

ROTATION OF CROPS

A simple definition of the phrase 'rotation of crops' would be a system by which vegetables of the same character do not follow one another on the same piece of ground year after year. You can classify vegetables in all kinds of ways: the botanist will do so by means of natural orders; the chemist might do so by means of the manures they particularly need; the gardener can do so by studying their root systems – deep-rooting crops versus shallow-rooting crops; crops that tend to clean the land well or to leave it rather dirty.

REASONS FOR ROTATIONS

It is said that plants give off from their roots what are known as toxins. These are not usually harmful to other plants, but an accumulation of them in the ground can prevent the perfect growth of plants of the same type that follow them. For instance, land can get what is known as 'strawberry sick', or 'cauliflower sick'. Land in this condition will not grow strawberries in the one case and cauliflowers in the other – at least, not successfully.

Fungus diseases that attack one crop may not attack another, and it would be foolish to plant the same type of crop in the same piece of ground year after year, just where the fungus disease was waiting to do it harm. The same is true of insect pests. Don't sow carrots in the same place where carrot fly was known to be last year. The pest will still be lurking there.

By growing celery in different parts of the garden, you ensure that all the land gets the benefit of the specially prepared celery trenches you have to dig. Thus your soil over a number of years is improved in depth and texture as a result of rotating your celery trenches. This is true of other cleaning crops as well. The widely different methods of cultivation needed by particular crops gives the ground a variety of treatments, provided these crops are grown in different parts of the garden each year. By moving the crops about, you do not allow the soil to deteriorate in the way it might if it got the same treatment year after year.

Some plants require one food out of the soil, while other plants require another. So, if you rotate your crops, what one plant does not use up is taken up by the crop that follows. But we mustn't make too much of this idea, as it should be possible, with compost, to make up for these deficiencies.

THREE-COURSE ROTATION

In this scheme the vegetable land is divided up – mentally, at least – into three plots: (1) for the roots, (2) for the cabbage family, and (3) for potatoes. Plot 1, has potatoes growing on it the first year, roots growing on it the second year, and the cabbage family growing on it the third year. The simple plan below will explain the idea.

	Year 1	Year 2	Year 3
Plot 1	Potatoes	Roots	Cabbages
Plot 2	Roots	Cabbages	Potatoes
Plot 3	Cabbages	Potatoes	Roots

In this way you will group together the crops that need similar treatment and have the same kind of requirements. Another aim is to make deep-rooting crops alternate with shallow-rooting vegetables. As far as possible 'families' are kept together. For this reason, we put turnips in with the cabbage family, as they are closely related and get the same diseases and pests – notably club root.

A three-course rotation is simple to use, but it is not very easy to fit in all crops. Gardeners are apt to wonder where to put such things as celery and leeks, for instance, but these can be used as dividing lines between the areas if necessary – and so can runner beans or peas, if desired. In some ways, then, the four-course rotation has its advantages.

FOUR-COURSE ROTATION

Here the land is divided up into four equal plots, and the vegetables are grouped into four sections also. Group A would be potatoes, Group B the pulse family (ie peas and beans), and in this group for convenience's sake we can include our celery, leeks, onions and shallots. Group C can be the root crops (ie carrots, parsnips, beetroot and unusual vegetables like salsify and scorzonera), and Group D the cabbage family (ie Brussels sprouts, savoys, cauliflowers, turnips and swedes, kale and kohlrabi); in this section, also, may be included spinach.

The crops that have been left out are either the permanent crops that must have a place all to themselves, so that they needn't be disturbed; plants like artichokes that grow very tall and so need growing at one end of the garden; dwarf plants, like parsley and chives, which make excellent edgings; and catch crops, like radish and lettuce, that can be grown almost anywhere.

Use the rotational system to its fullest advantage. It will help you rotate your systems of manuring and your systems of cultivation, and will save you time and labour in the long run. You may also find that rotations save you money.

11 Vegetables – roots and tubers

TUBEROUS CROPS

Quite a small group really, but a very important one. There are only two that we need consider – the potato and the Jerusalem artichoke.

POTATOES

Perhaps this is the most important crop in the garden.

Soil. Nearly all soils are suitable for potatoes, though clays and peaty soils produce tubers which are commonly called 'soapy'. The best preparation for potatoes is to cover the land with rotted compost in late autumn. The rows should run north and south, if possible. As soon as possible after the beginning of March rake the soil over to bring it down to a fine tilth.

Seed. Be sure you buy Certified seed from Scotland or Ireland, or even Wales. It always gives heavier crops, and you can purchase Scotch or Irish seed from your local garden supplier, who will give you the necessary guarantee. Do not try and save your own seed or buy it from neighbours. The seed tubers should weigh about $2\frac{1}{2}$ oz and should be about the size of a hen's egg. If you have to buy large tubers, plant them directly they are cut. When cutting a tuber in two, make sure each portion has at least one 'eye'.

Sprouting. Potatoes do best if they are sprouted in trays before being put into the ground. A potato has two ends, known as the rose end and the heel. The rose is the end that has the most eyes, and will always be found at the opposite end to the part that was attached to the root. Stand the tubers rose-end upwards in a shallow wooden tray (you can buy purpose-made trays, or knock them together yourself). A potato tray is normally 2 ft 6 ins long, 1 ft 6 ins wide, and $3\frac{1}{2}$ ins deep, and has corner posts standing 3 ins above the sides. This allows the trays to be stood one above the other while the sprouting process is going on. Put the trays anywhere where they will be free from frost, and where there will be plenty of light. Air should circulate freely among them as well. Some time afterwards shoots will grow and, if too many arise from the same tuber, you can rub out all except one or two. A good 'sprit' should be stout, strong and dark green, and not longer than 2 ins. Spritting ensures the potatoes being several weeks earlier than if they were left unsprouted. Heavier crops result as well.

General cultivation. It is difficult to dictate about distances between the rows and distances between the plants themselves. Roughly speaking, the very earlies on a south border should be planted with the rows 18 ins apart and the tubers 1 ft apart in the rows. Normally the distances advised are: first earlies, 1 ft 9 ins × 1 ft, second earlies, 2 ft 3ins × 1 ft 3 ins, and main crops 2 ft 6ins × 1 ft 6ins. You can alter the distances to suit varieties and soils, and these distances are merely a guide. Never plant deeper than 2 or 3 ins; any necessary extra depth is added by applying more compost. Place the seed carefully in a hole made with a trowel, to avoid injuring the sprits. A handful of grass mowings may be put over each potato, to prevent them from becoming scabby. The compost is then drawn over, leaving a very slight ridge to mark the row.

In some districts it is possible to plant in the middle of March, but north of the potteries mid-April is more usual. When the plants are about 8 ins high, more compost should be raked up to them with a hoe, making a ridge say 5 ins high. This encourages the plants to throw tubers. Further earthing up or applications of compost may be done in a few weeks' time to bring the soil up yet another inch.

Manuring. In addition to the dressing of compost which should be at the rate of one good barrowload to 10 sq. yds, fish fertilizer should be applied at 3 oz per square yard. It is usually useless to give fish manure to early potatoes as they are out of the ground before they can make use of these plant foods.

Storing. Early potatoes can be dug up as soon as they are fit to use. The main crops should be left in the ground until the haulm has died down. They should then be lifted carefully and stored. A shed or cellar is quite suitable, but they can also be kept in burys or clamps. These are made in a convenient piece of dry ground – put down a 3-in. layer of straw, put the potatoes in a mound on the straw, and then cover them over with more straw and, finally, soil. To ventilate the clamp poke in a twist of straw to peep out at the top.

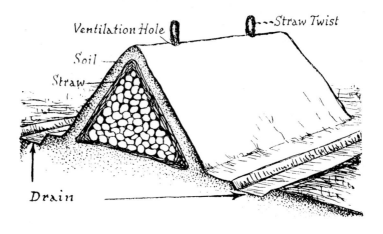

A potato clamp

Pests and diseases. Unfortunately there are large numbers of these. The commonest is blight (phytophthorainfestans), which can be controlled by spraying with Bordeaux mixture. Common scab (actinomyces scabies) is seen on the tuber in little scabby spots. If plenty of lawn mowings are put into the drills at planting time, this disease should be prevented.

Varieties

Earlies

Suttons Foremost	Very heavy cropper, white, oval.
Arran Pilot	White, long.
Di Vernon	Purple-eyed, long.

Second earlies

Catriona	Purple-eyed, long variety.
Craigs Royal	Pink-eyed, oval.
Maris Peer	White, oval.

Main crops

Majestic	Large, white and long.
Dr McIntosh	White, long.
Kerr's Pink	Pink and round.

Special note. If you own land that is subject to wart disease remember there is no known cure for it. You are bound by law to grow what are known as immune varieties. The following are immune: Ally, Arran Comrade, Great Scott, King George, Kerr's Pink, Majestic, Arran Pilot, Gladstone, Arran Crest.

JERUSALEM ARTICHOKE

One of the most easily grown vegetables in the garden. It will grow practically anywhere, though you cannot expect large tubers of good quality if you plant them in an odd neglected corner.

Planting. The tubers are planted any time from February to the beginning of April, the rows being 2 ft 6ins apart, and the tubers 12 ins in the rows. They grow to a height of 6 ft or more, and will provide quite a good screen at the bottom of the garden. See that the tubers are put about 6 ins deep in the ground.

Manuring. As for potatoes.

General cultivation. Hoe along the rows from time to time, to keep down weeds and to provide a mulch, but do not earth up.

Lifting. Directly the tops have died down, the roots may be lifted and stored in sand. On the other hand, they can be left in the ground, as they are not affected by frost, and so can be used as desired. Dig up every single tuber, as if even the smallest one is left in, it will grow the next year.

Varieties. Grow the Fuseau variety as it is free from knobs on the tubers.

ROOT CROPS

All root crops need well-prepared soil, but they dislike fresh manure. If you want to get a good, clean, straight root, you must not manure with dung. When fresh manure is used, the roots always fork. Be very careful not to damage the roots while hoeing, as otherwise they may go to seed. In fact, anything that checks growth – excessive drought, too much rain, attempts at transplanting – all have the same effect. Root crops need phosphates and potash, and little nitrogen.

BEETROOT

You should aim to grow beet that are not too coarse, and that when cut, are free from white rings. The root should be crimson right the way through. Beet bleed very easily, and should not be damaged during cultivation or lifting.

Soil. The best soil for beet is probably a light and sandy one, though good roots can be grown in clays, provided they are well drained.

Seed sowing. The seed should be sown at the end of April or the beginning of May, though in heavy clay soils sowing should be deferred a fortnight. The drills should be 12 ins apart, 2 ins deep, and the plants should be thinned out finally to 8 ins apart. It is usual to thin beetroot at two periods – first, when they are a few inches high, to 4 ins apart, and then, when they are fit for use, to 8 ins apart.

Cultivation. Hoe between the rows. If any part of the row fails, it is possible to transplant, especially if the weather is showery or if plenty of water can be given.

Manuring. On light land salt may be given, at the rate of 2 oz per square yard, when the plants are half grown. A fish or seaweed manure should be applied a week or ten days before sowing the seed, at the rate of 4 oz to the square yard.

Storing. Lift carefully, and store in a clamp in the same way as potatoes, or in dry earth or sand in a shed. The beet must be dug up before the winter frosts, and this usually means the middle of October. The roots will usually keep in good condition until the following June.

Varieties

Round

Boltardy	Sweet, fresh, never runs to seed.
Detroit	Rich maroon colour, uniform at harvesting.

Long

Long Blood Red Covent Garden	Handsome, long beet with a small top.

Yellow

Golden Beet	Gorgeous flavour, a honeycomb colour.

CARROTS

As with potatoes, there are early varieties and main crops, but there are also round-rooted types, intermediate types, and some which have long, red roots.

Soil. Carrots do best on a deep, sandy loam. If you have heavy soil, then you had better grow the short or stump-rooted varieties. The earliest carrots are produced by sowing about mid-March on a specially prepared, warm, dry border into which sedge peat has been raked liberally. Do not sow if the soil is wet and cold, but wait for warmer weather. The drills should be 6 ins apart. When the plants are up, they should be thinned out to 2 ins apart. Another sowing may be made at the beginning of April.

Seed sowing. Under ordinary cultivation, drills are made about $\frac{3}{4}$ in. deep and 12 to 18 ins apart, according to the variety. For small gardens the intermediate varieties are most useful.

Cultivation. As soon as the seedlings are large enough to handle, thin them out with a draw hoe to 3 ins apart, the final thinning being done by hand, either to 4 ins or 6 ins apart, according to the variety. The thinnings should not be left about, but should be taken away and composted to help prevent carrot fly attack. Immediately after thinning, draw the soil up to the row. Then spray with garlic oil (1 teaspoonful to a gallon of water) and fill the spaces up where the roots have been removed. Continue hoeing throughout the summer until the soil is fully mulched with powdery compost or sedge peat, when hoeing will be largely unnecessary.

Manuring. For early varieties 2 oz of fish manure per square yard will do, though if growth does not seem quick enough, waterings with a liquid manure may be given occasionally as well. For main crops use the same fertilizers as recommended for beetroot.

Storing. Carrot roots should be lifted and stored as for beetroot.

Pests and diseases. The carrot fly is the most common, and preventive methods should be used, as previously outlined. In addition, burn all the roots that have been attacked and use whizzed naphthalene along the rows after thinning, at about 1 oz to the yard run.

Varieties

Shorthorns: Nantes; Kurna; Early Gem.

Intermediate: James' Scarlet Intermediate.

Maincrop – half long: Chantenay; Red Cored; Autumn King; Vitalonga.

PARSNIPS
Perhaps the easiest of all root vegetables to grow.

Soil. Parsnips will do in any type of soil provided it is not too stony. To grow large, well-shaped roots, bore a conical hole 3 ft deep and 3 ins in diameter at the top. Fill this up with friable, sifted soil, and sow two or three seeds on the top. Thin out to one plant when the seedlings grow.

Seed sowing. Parsnips can be sown at the end of February or the beginning of March, provided the ground is dry enough. Parsnip seeds should be sown thickly, as only about half will germinate, as a rule. The rows should be 18 ins apart and the drills $\frac{1}{2}$ in. deep. When the seedlings are 1 in. or so high, thin them to 8 ins apart.

Cultivation. Hoe to keep down weeds and to ensure a dust mulch, unless you have mulched liberally with powdery compost or sedge peat.

Storing. There is no need to store parsnips; they can be left in the ground until they are required. In fact, parsnips always taste better after they have had some frost on them. If you are in a district which normally has hard winters, dig some of your parsnips and store them. It is very annoying to know you have got parsnips in the ground but, because the soil is frozen, you cannot dig them.

Pests and diseases. The celery fly sometimes attacks parsnip leaves and may do some harm. Canker is bad in some soils, but a variety that is almost immune is Avon Resister.

Varieties Improved Hollow Crown; The Student and Avon Resister.

TURNIPS

Turnips should really be grown with the cabbage family, because they truly belong to it and are liable to the same pests and diseases.

Soil. They are not very particular as to soil, though a sandy loam is said to grow them better than heavier soils. They are very difficult to grow on shallow soils over chalk, as these do not retain moisture easily. Roots on droughty soils lacking in humus seem to be more readily attacked by the turnip flea beetle and run to seed easily.

Seed sowing. Turnips may be sown during the early part of March in a sheltered spot, provided the ground is dry enough to get down to a fine tilth. Such sowing is usually done broadcast, and thinning is done to roughly 4 ins apart when the plants are large enough to handle. Later sowings are made in drills 12 ins apart, the turnips being thinned to 6 ins apart in the rows.

The main late summer supply is obtained by sowing in May, preferably in a shady situation, while seed for autumn and winter crops is sown from the middle of July to the end of August. The drills for winter turnips are 18 ins apart, the first thinning being to 6 ins, and the final thinning being to 12 ins, for the roots that are being left to stand throughout the winter.

Some people like turnip tops as a green vegetable, and, if so, sowings are made early in September in rows 2 ft apart. No thinning is carried out.

Cultivation. Hoe the ground regularly, unless the land is well mulched with powdery compost or sedge peat.

Manuring. Rake in powdery compost at two large bucketfuls to the square yard. This helps to retain the soil moisture and prevents bolting. If the turnip is being grown as a catch crop the organic manuring given to the previous vegetable will often be adequate. The fertilizer recommended for beetroot may be given, but don't forget that the turnip is a lime lover. A top dressing of lime at 4 oz per square yard just before sowing the seed usually helps matters considerably.

Storing. In normal winters the roots may stand outdoors. But in districts subject to sharp frosts the roots would be spoiled, and should be lifted and clamped as for potatoes.

Pests and diseases. The turnip flea beetle attacks the leaves, gradually eating them away. Dusting with derris is quite a good control. Do not allow weeds like shepherd's purse and charlock to grow, as these are alternative hosts. The maggot of the turnip gall weevil will be found inside the gall on the root, and people often confuse this with club root, though turnips can also be attacked with club root disease.

Varieties
Frame. Early Long White Frame: has a blunt nose and minute tap-root, being very tender. Jersey Navet is a little shorter. These varieties can be sown in frames early in February if a hot-bed has been prepared.

Summer. Early Snowball; Early White Stone; Golden Ball; Jersey Lily – the epicure variety. In this case the seed is sown outside from March onwards.

Winter. Chirk Castle; Veitch's Red Globe – a quick-growing yet hardy sort; Manchester Market: a delicious type.

SALSIFY

A very delicious vegetable that is not grown enough by amateur gardeners. It is often known popularly as the vegetable oyster.

Soil. Possibly the best soil for salsify is a deep, well-worked light loam. Salsify will grow quite well in a heavy soil, especially if ridged in the autumn.

Seed sowing. The seed should not be sown until April, the drills being 12 ins apart and 1 in. deep. As soon as the seedlings can be handled, they should be thinned out to 4 ins apart, and finally to 8 ins apart.

Cultivation. Hoe continuously to keep the surface soil crumbly, or cover the ground along the rows with powdery compost or sedge peat.

Manuring. No dung or compost should be forked in when the land is prepared, but salsify will grow best if it follows a well-manured crop. The organic fertilizers recommended for all root crops should be applied fourteen days or so before sowing the seed required. They can be dug up, and stored in moist sand in a shed, but if this is done they must be handled with care as they bleed easily.

Pests and diseases. This crop is practically free from pests and diseases.

Varieties. Mammoth Sandwich Island: very delicious.

12 Vegetables – brassicas, peas and beans

THE BRASSICA FAMILY

The brassica family includes practically all the green crops that are grown for the table. All members of the brassica family are subject to club root, and this is one of the reasons why it is necessary to carry out rotation of crops. Lime will not only prevent the land getting too acid, but will act as a deterrent against this disease. Lime should always be applied before planting out the members of this family.

Nitrogen is a necessary factor in the successful cultivation of all such crops, and in addition to the compost other organic fertilizers like fish manure should be given.

KALE OR BORECOLE

This is a hardy winter vegetable which can be cut and cut again. It is certainly a vegetable to grow in hard winters, as frost seems to improve the quality.

Soil. Kale will grow in practically any soil, though perhaps the heavier soils suit them best.

Seeds. Seeds are sown at the beginning of April, in a seed bed, and, if the young plants grow too thickly they can be thinned out when 2 ins high.

Cultivation. The plants can be put out during June and July, either between other crops or in rows on their own. The distance apart depends on the variety, the smaller types needing 2 ft × 2 ft, and the taller varieties 3 ft × 2 ft 6ins. Little cultivation between this crop is necessary once winter has set in.

Manuring. Do not compost too heavily, or the plants will grow soft and luxuriant, and so be damaged by frosts and cold winds. No dung should be given, but a complete organic fertilizer like fish manure may be used at 3–4 oz to the square yard.

Varieties. There are a very large number of varieties and types of kale. You can have tall or dwarf ones or even curly ones.

The Cottager's Kale is hardy and prolific; A1 is densely curled and compact; while there is a Green-Curled Dwarf and a Green-Curled Tall. Asparagus Kale has distinctive long, thin shoots. Hungry Gap Kale is sown in June for cropping May–June the following year.

BROCCOLI

This is, of course, the winter cauliflower. It is not perhaps quite so tender as its prototype, but it is very useful to have a nice supply of it throughout the winter.

Soil. Broccoli seems to prefer a heavy loam. It is very important to see that the soil is firm, as rich, loose soil only produces loose, open hearts. On light land it will be necessary to add compost after having firmed the ground down and before the plants are put in.

Seed sowing. The seed is sown in shallow drills, 9 ins apart, on a specially prepared, friable bed. If you want good heads in the autumn, sow at the end of March. Winter varieties should be sown at the end of April or the beginning of May, while for the varieties that will be cut in May and early June the following year, the seed should be put in in the middle of May. Never let broccoli plants get thin and leggy, so thin out the seedlings early in their growth. It is not a bad plan to take out the best plants and transplant them into another seed bed 3 ins apart. Keep the seed bed and the transplanted bed free from weeds.

Cultivation. It is convenient to use broccoli as a crop to follow potatoes, dwarf beans or peas. The ground has then been well manured and yet had time to settle down and to be firm. Put the plants out with 2 ft 6 ins between the rows, and 2 ft in the rows. If possible do this on a showery day, and, if not, water the plants in.

As the plants get ready to cut, if you want to keep the curds perfectly white, bend one of the leaves over the top, breaking it if necessary to keep it in position.

In hard winters it is a good plan to heel the plants over to the north. A spadeful of soil can be taken out on the north side of the plant, so that the plant can easily be bent over. What injures the curd is not so much the frost, but alternate frost and thaw. Heeling over helps to prevent this.

Manuring. Don't give large quantities of compost unless the soil is really starved. It is far better to manure the previous crop more heavily than normal, to leave the ground rich enough for broccoli. Apply 3 oz of fish manure to the square yard before planting.

Varieties. Broccoli varieties can be divided into three divisions:

First Division
Extra Early Roscoff: cuts late November.
Winter Mammoth: cuts in November and December.

Second Division
Early Feltham: cuts mid-January and early February.
Early White: cuts in March.
Armado April: cuts in April.

Third Division
Armado Tardo: cuts in May.
Late Queen: cuts end of May and early June.

SPROUTING BROCCOLI
This can be grown in the same way as broccoli. It does not produce a white curd, but a large number of green leaves and tender flowering stems. These are cut off before the flowers open, while they are still immature, and are very delicious.

Varieties. For Christmas week, Calabrese Green Sprouting is useful. Early Purple Sprouting for April, Late Purple Sprouting for April–May.

BRUSSELS SPROUTS
With care it should be possible to pick Brussels sprouts from September until March. To grow them well there are four points to remember: (1) they need a long season of growth, (2) they need plenty of room for development, (3) they must be heavily fed, and (4) firm ground is an absolute necessity.

Soil. Sprouts are not particular about soil, though they usually crop more heavily on clay than on sand.

Seed sowing. To obtain succession, it is a good plan to sow batches of seed at various periods of the year. The first sowing can be made in August in a sheltered border, the plants 3 ins apart. Another sowing can be made in a frame early in February, or sowings can be made outside during March. The seed bed should consist of light, rich soil in a sheltered position. When the spring-sown seedlings are fit to handle they should

Brussels sprout F1 hybrid 'Fasolt'

be transplanted into further seed beds at 3 ins square. Pick out the largest plants the first time, and then go over the original bed again a fortnight later, and pick out the largest of those that are left, and so on. Successive batches of plants can be obtained in this way from one sowing.

Cultivation. The sturdy plants that you have by now produced are planted out at least $2\frac{1}{2}$ ft square during May, or perhaps even early June. Some of the taller and more prolific varieties actually need 3 ft square. Plant during a showery period, or water the plants in. If you want, you can grow catch crops in between the sprout rows. Whatever you do, see that the ground is firm before planting. Loose, open sprouts are produced otherwise.

When the sprouts are ready to gather cut them off leaving a very short stalk on the main stem. In this way further sprouts are encouraged, which lengthens the season. Hoeing will be necessary to keep down weeds and to provide a dust mulch. As the main leaves turn yellow, they can be removed with a knife, but don't cut off the large leaves while they are still green.

The head should not be removed until the end of February, as this helps the plant in sprout formation and protects the plant as a whole.

Manuring. Brussels sprouts are always hungry, so add compost liberally as a top dressing when you are preparing the ground. In addition, a fortnight or so before putting the plants out, sprinkle fish manure or meat bonemeal over the soil, at 3 oz to the square yard. Don't forget a dressing of lime at 5 oz per square yard if, on testing, you find that the soil is acid.

Varieties

Timperley Champion	Tall variety	A good keeper
Cambridge Early	Large size	Solid sprouts
Clucas Favourite	Tall	Studded with solid sprouts
King Arthur	Fairy tall	Medium sized dark green sprouts
Prince Askold	Semi-tall	Heavy crops of medium sized sprouts
Early Half Tall	Not tall	Large sprouts of good quality
Irish Elegance	Tall	Good yields of high quality sprouts
Roodnerf Seven Hills		Small, tight first quality sprouts

Special note. Take notice of the points mentioned in the first paragraph, especially the one about plenty of room for development. You cannot give Brussels sprouts too much room!

CABBAGE

There are cabbages for summer, cabbages for spring, and nice-firm-hearted ones for winter. You ought to be able to get a supply of good cabbages all the year round.

Soil. Provided you can add organic manure or, better still, compost in November for the worms to pull in, cabbages will grow well on almost any land. If they do prefer one soil more than another, it is a retentive loam.

Seed sowing. Spring cabbage is usually sown in July, or in the warm south-west in August. Rake the ground down to a fine tilth, and sow the seed thinly in drills 9 ins apart and $\frac{1}{2}$ in. deep. Thin sowing makes it possible for you to leave the plants in the seed-bed until they have to be put out in September. Of course, sturdier plants do result if you transplant them when they are fit to handle into another prepared bed.

Summer cabbage, sown in March, and, if you like, at fortnightly intervals afterwards, can provide plants which may be planted directly there is any vacant land.

Winter cabbage is sown in April or May, though in the north it is often sown in March with the summer varieties.

A well-hearted cabbage

General mote. The method of sowing and planting for summer and winter cabbage are the same as for spring cabbage.

Cultivation. Spring cabbages (as they are fairly small and will be cut early) can be planted with 18 ins between the rows and 12 ins between the plants. Summer cabbages can be planted with 2 ft between the rows and 18 ins in the rows, while some of the large drumhead winter cabbages may need 2 ft square.

The ground should be limed, if it is at all acid, using 5–7 oz of hydrated lime to the square yard. Hoe between the rows if you are not adopting the compost mulching method. The stalks should be removed from the ground as soon as possible after the cabbages are cut; bash them up with the back of an axe and put them on the compost heap. Use an organic activator on the compost heap.

Manuring. Cabbages, like Brussels sprouts, are gross feeders, and, except in the case of spring cabbages, the ground should be well manured. Also apply 3 oz of fish manure or use a meat and bone meal instead. In very light soils you can use wood ashes at 7 oz to the square yard. With September-planted spring cabbage bonemeal may be used, especially on heavy land, at 5 oz to the square yard.

Varieties

Spring cabbages
First Early 218: one of the best early cabbages in cultivation.
Flower of Spring: firm hearts, few outside leaves.
Durham Elf: dark green; a large cabbage.
Wheeler's Imperial: noted for its flavour.

Summer cabbages
Primo: early, dwarf and compact, 'cut' in July and August.
Holland Winter: large, firm round heads.
Winningstadt: conical, pointed heads.
Hispi: compact, pointed heart.

Winter cabbages
Golden Acre: ball-like heart.
Christmas Drumhead: drum-like heart.

RED PICKLING CABBAGE

This can be sown the first week in August in exactly the same way as for any other kind of cabbage. The manuring and cultivation are similar also.

Varieties
Red Drumhead: early, good-sized firm hearts.
Lydiate: red drumhead; large and late.
Ruby Red: the earliest for spring sowing.

KOHLRABI

This is a cross between a turnip and a cabbage. A large turnip-like stem is produced above the ground, with leaves

Kohl-rabi, 'White Vienna'

growing all round it. The side leaves gradually fall off, and the roots can be used any time throughout the winter. Kohl-rabi is perfectly hardy, and is an excellent crop to grow in dry years.

The seed is sown outdoors, where the plants are to grow, at any time from the beginning of April until the end of June. The seedlings are thinned out to 9 ins apart, and can be transplanted if necessary. Manure as for cabbages.

Varieties. Green Vienna: small and delicious. There is also a large purple type.

SAVOYS

The savoy has deeply crinkled leaves, is extremely hardy, and is used throughout the winter. Frost does not spoil the plants, but actually improves the flavour.

Soil. Savoys prefer heavy, rich land, and can follow crops like potatoes and peas.

Seed sowing. The seed is usually sown in three batches: in the middle of March, at the beginning of April, and a final sowing at the end of April. The seedlings are thinned out early, the drills 8 ins apart. Keep the rows clean and free from weeds.

Cultivation. Put the plants out into their permanent position during June and July, and on showery days if possible. The smallest varieties only need 17 ins between the rows and 15 ins in the rows. The larger varieties need planting 2 ft square.

Manuring. After the previous crop has been cleared, it is quite a good plan to cover the ground with brown, powdery compost or sedge peat at 9 oz to the square yard. But first rake in 4 oz of a good fish manure per square yard.

Varieties
Best of All: large, early; ready late in October.
Dwarf Green Curled: compact, medium sized and hardy.
Early drumhead: reliable very large variety with solid hearts.
Ice Queen: solid, uniform hearts of excellent quality; hardy.
Ormskirk Late: large headed and exceedingly hardy.
Savoy King: uniform, vigorous and high-yielding.

THE PULSE FAMILY

This is a very large family of pod-bearing vegetables, all of which have on their roots nodules containing bacteria which live in harmony with the plant. These are able to make use of nitrogen from the atmosphere. If the roots are left in the ground when the crop is cleared, much nitrogenous plant food is left behind. They should not be given any nitrogenous fertilizers in the early stages. Lime should always be applied on any but calcareous soils at the rate of $\frac{1}{4}$ lb per square yard before sowing the seed.

PEAS

There are all kinds of peas – not only tall and dwarf varieties, early and late ones, but special types, like sugar peas or asparagus peas.

Soil. Peas will grow on most soils, though those that are light and sandy seem to suit them best. The later varieties prefer a retentive loam that has been well drained.

Seed sowing. Prepare the ground for peas in the autumn by applying compost all over the soil at one good barrowload to 8 sq. yds, and leaving it rough. In this way it will be pulled into the soil by the worms which leads to a fine tilth in the spring. Draw drills out 5 ins wide, and 2–3 ins deep; the distance between the rows should be equal to the height of the variety sown.

If you want a succession of green peas from, say, the beginning of June to the end of October, you will have to make a large number of sowings throughout the year. The earliest crops come, of course, from sowings made under cloches or access frames.

In the south and west peas are normally sown at the beginning of November, out of doors in a sheltered situation. These peas may have to be protected if heavy frosts occur, and so it is a good plan to stick them early, and, before and during frosty periods, to place straw along the rows. November sowings do best on light soils. Draw the drill out in the morning, to let it dry out a little, and then sow the seed in the afternoon.

The next showing might be made at the beginning of February, though in the midlands and north it is safest to wait until the end of March. From the beginning of April onwards make another sowing as soon as the last one is showing well above the ground.

Roughly speaking, the early varieties will be sown in November, February and March, and, of course, again if necessary in June. The second earliest are sown in April and the main crop in May.

General cultivation. You cannot grow good peas unless you are prepared to keep the ground clean either by hoeing or by applying powdery compost or sedge peat. Moisture is absolutely essential, and mulchings should be given. Lawn mowings can be put along the rows early in June, but never deeper than $\frac{1}{2}$ in. If watering has to be carried out, it should not be done on the row itself, but in small trenches on either side of the row. The ground should be soaked and not just dampened.

All peas should be 'sticked'* if possible, though the dwarf 18-in. types will grow quite well without support. Place the peasticks 6 ins away from the peas, and 1 ft away from one another. They should be put in at an angle of 45 degrees; the angle on one side being opposite to the angle on the other. In this way the sticks can support one another. Small, twiggy pieces of stick can be inserted in the ground near the peas to encourage the plants to climb upwards. Some people use wire netting instead, stretched along the row.

Pick peas regularly, as one pod left on to ripen and to go to seed will immediately reduce the cropping powers of that plant. Regular picking helps heavy cropping.

*When pea sticks are not available wire netting can be used

Manuring. Compost should be applied in autumn rather than in spring. Just before sowing, fork in 5 oz of meat and bone-meal or fish manure per square yard – potash may be given in addition, ie wood ashes at 8 oz to the square yard. As soon as the plants are through dried blood may be applied at 1 oz per yard run.

Varieties. It is very difficult to make a selection from the large number of varieties of peas offered by seed firms. I have found that the following crop heavily:

Dwarf earlies

Kelvedon Wonder	1½ ft	Wrinkle seeded.
Feltham First	1½ ft	Earliest pea.
Little Marvel	18 ins	Best flavoured early pea.
Laxton's Superb	2½ ft	Good for sowing in autumn or January.

Early main crop

Early Onward	2 ft	Compact grower, heavy cropper.
Gradus	2½ ft	Very large pods.

Main crops

Onward	2½ ft	Resistant to mildew. Good flavour, heavy cropper.
Gladstone	4 ft	Full pods.
Johnson's Freezer	2 ft	An excellent freezing variety.

Late Variety

Alderman	5 ft

General remarks. To keep away mice and birds soak the peas in a mixture of paraffin and red lead for a couple of hours before sowing. This liquid should be about the consistency of cream. To get earlier peas, pinch out the growing points, but the plants will not grow so tall.

BROAD BEANS

To get earlier peas, pinch out the growing points, and the plants will not grow so tall.

Soil. They are not particular as to soil, and will grow well almost anywhere. They do like deep, moist soil, however.

Seed sowing. The first sowing is done in November, the rows 2 ft 6 ins apart. A drill is made 3 ins deep, 6 ins or so wide, and a double row of beans put in 6 ins apart. Double rows are usually better than single rows; as the beans will not be prevented from cropping heavily, a heavier yield is obtained from the same area of ground when compared to single rows.

To obtain succession you can sow outdoors again at the beginning of February, and again early in March. Some people like to raise the plants in a frame, from seed sown at the beginning of December. The plants thus raised are put out early in March. When sowing beans outside, it is a good plan to sow a dozen or so extra beans in a group at the end of the row, which may be planted out into the row when they are 3 ins high, if any blanks occur.

General cultivation. When the plants are 3–4 ins high, the soil should be drawn up to them during hoeing. After this, carry out regular surface cultivation. Keep a lookout for black fly, and, to prevent it damaging the crop, pinch out the growing point directly the first blossom has set and spray the plants with liquid derris.

Manuring. See peas.

Varieties
Aquadulce: very early; enormous pods.
Green Windsor: a green seeded bean of excellent flavour.
Bunyards Long Pod: a large-podded variety.
Threefold White: excellent for freezing; the pods are 6–7 ins long; the beans themselves are smaller than other varieties.

DWARF BEANS
Dwarf beans are given all kinds of names, sometimes being called kidney beans and sometimes French beans. They are often grown under glass. You cannot sow dwarf beans until the ground is really warm. They need a temperature of about 60 degrees F before they will germinate properly.

Soil. A light soil suits them better than a heavy one. Clays and heavy loams should be 'lightened' with any material available.

Seed sowing. It is impossible to sow the seed outside much earlier than April, and it is often the first week in May before the soil is ready in many gardens. The drills should be 2 ins deep, 4 ins wide, and 2–3 ft apart, depending on the variety. The beans themselves should be put into the rows by hand, in a staggered formation, so that the plants grow 6 ins apart.

A dozen or more beans are then planted at the end of the row to cope with any gaps that arise. To get earlier beans than this, you can sow in February in boxes or pots under glass. About the middle of March the plants should be hardened off, and planted out during the last week of April.

Seed can also be sown in frames, 2 ins apart, early in April, and these will be ready to put out the second week in May. When sowing in frames, be sure to protect them from frost at night; remember they are very soft and can be cut down easily.

Cultivation. It is customary to sow French beans in between another crop like spring cabbage or autumn-sown lettuce. The advantage here is that the established crop gives some protection to the young beans when they come through, and the mycorrhiza on the roots of the one crop help those on the roots of the other crop. The original crop is cleared by the time the beans require the room, and so space and time are saved. As soon as the previous crop is out of the way, rake the ground over between the rows.

Whatever you do, keep picking all the time. Don't be tempted to leave the pods on until they are old and stringy.

Manuring. The beans will be sown on ground that has been well treated before, and all they should require is a dressing of lime. Broadcast a good fish manure or meat and bonemeal where the rows are to be, ten days or so before making out the drills. If growth is slow when the protected crop has disappeared, you can give $\frac{1}{2}$ oz dried blood per yard run along the rows.

Varieties
The Prince: heavy cropper, early, oustanding.
Flair: very dwarf, quick in growth, stringless.
Masterpiece: long pods, heavy cropper, early.
Pencil Pod Black Wax: heavy cropper, tender, pods golden yellow.

RUNNER BEANS
Most garden owners like to grow a few runner beans, and, as they look quite decorative, they are often grown as a division between the vegetable garden and flower garden, at the end of the garden to screen off refuse heaps or to clamber up the fence.

Soil. As with all members of this family, a light loam is preferable to a heavy clay. Undrained clays are a real danger.

Seed sowing. Runner beans are less hardy than dwarf beans, and it is impossible to sow the seed any earlier than the beginning of May. If necessary, another sowing may be made in June. Runner beans can be grown up poles, string, wire netting, or on the flat, the trailing growths being cut back with a sickle to keep the plants bushy. Some people grow them in rows, while others put three poles into the ground to form a triangle and the beans climb up these.

If you are growing the beans up some structure and in rows, you will need to have them about 6 ft apart. Most people sow double rows, 3 ins deep and 9 ins apart. Put the seed 9 ins apart in each drill, on the staggered or alternate method. If poles are used, put them in a foot apart between the two drills, and on each side. The poles cross at the top by about 6 ins, and a series of poles are now laid on the top where the sticks cross, and the whole thing lashed tightly together. This makes a very firm structure. If you are growing on the flat, the rows are just sown $3\frac{1}{2}$–4 ft apart, the seeds being sown 8 ins apart in the rows.

Cultivation. When the seeds start to grow, the soil should be stirred lightly. When the plants are 3–4 ins high a little soil may be drawn up to them.

Beans grown on the flat are cut back regularly with a pair of shears. In dry seasons it is a good plan to syringe the plants either early in the morning or at night-time. This helps the flowers to set, and keeps the pods fresh. Pick the plants over regularly, and do not miss any that are fit to use.

Manuring. Quite heavy manuring with compost or other organic material like sedge peat is advisable. Add a good fish manure or meat and bonemeal at 3–4 oz per square yard. This can be raked into the ground a week before sowing the seed. Lime will be needed, also, on the surface of the ground, using about 3 oz per square yard.

Varieties
Emperor: long pods, fine quality.
Princeps: early and dwarf, heavy cropping.
Czar: white flowers; broad pods.
East Anglian Champion: stringless; much liked by cooks.

13 Vegetables – celery, onions, asparagus, spinach, rhubarb, leeks and marrows

I have grouped these vegetables together largely because they usually have deeper cultivation. The only exception, perhaps, is spinach, and this may be regarded as a catch crop.

Celery, leeks and onions do need well-prepared ground, and asparagus and rhubarb are, of course, permanent crops. If you include spinach beet and seakale spinach, you will then have two more crops that will remain in the ground for over a year.

CELERY
Most people like celery either as a salad or as a cooked vegetable. There are many types that can be grown, such as the self-bleaching, the American and the pink and white. I am often told that celery is a nuisance because the plants have to be raised in a greenhouse in slight heat. This is not quite true, as celery seedlings can be raised in frames.

SOIL
Celery soil should have plenty of organic matter present and, curiously enough, acid soils grow celery better than those that have a lime content. It should be possible for these plants to obtain water throughout the season, and so soil with a fairly high watertable is useful.

SEED SOWING
It is best to have a 'hot bed' in a frame, 6 × 4 ft, and this is done by putting in an electric heating cable about 3 ins deep. Over this place Alex Soilless compost 1 in. deep, ie when trodden down and raked level. The seed is then sown in this layer.

Half an ounce of celery seed should sow a frame light of this size, though few people will need anywhere near this amount of seed. If you choose to use your frame for raising other plants at the same time, you can raise your celery plants in a corner of the frame, or, if you prefer, sow the seed in boxes, which you sink into the frame to at least half their depth.

After sowing, cover the seed lightly with soil, pressing it down with a board and watering it well. Shut the frame immediately, and, if it is likely to be frosty, cover the frame up at night-time with old sacks. As soon as the seedlings appear, a little air can be given in the day-time, and the amount of air given can be increased until by the middle of April the lights are taken off during the mild days, though it may be necessary to replace them at night. When the plants are 2 ins high prick them out 3 ins apart into a cold frame. Water them well and close the frame, and shade it until the young plants have rooted again. Be careful not to get them frozen either, so cover the frame up at night.

If you want very early crops – that is, celery that you will use in August – you will have to make your first sowing late in February. For ordinary work the middle of March will do, and the seedlings produced are usually transplanted in the rows 6 ins apart, though the plants are 3 ins apart in the rows. For very late crops delay sowing until the second week in April, pricking out the plants as before.

The general rules with regard to these seedlings are (1) they must always receive plenty of water, (2) they must never be frozen or receive any check at all, (3) the soil they grow in should always be full of organic material, to allow free root run, and (4) be careful not to let celery fly attack the young plants in the frame. It may be necessary to spray with nicotine even when they are seedlings.

GENERAL CULTIVATION

When lifting the plants from the frames, take care to remove them with as much root as possible; a trowel or a spade should be used.

The self-bleaching and American varieties of celery can be grown on the flat, and, to help them to blanch, straw may be placed around them. Self-bleaching celery need not be planted further apart than 1 ft square, or at the most 18 ins, as the plants do not grow very tall.

Ordinary celery is grown in trenches, which should be specially prepared. Dig down 18 ins, making a trench 18 ins wide. If you throw the excavated soil up on either side in equal proportions, you should end up with two ridges of equal height. To allow for this it is usual to have at least 2 ft 6 ins in between each trench. It is possible to have wider trenches than this, so that two or three rows may be grown in the one excavation. For every extra row you want to grow you will have to dig a trench 6 ins wider. It is not a bad plan to stick to the single trench if you can. In the bottom of the trench, place a layer of well-made compost, at least 6 ins deep when trodden down, and cover this with about 5 ins of soil. You should now have a trench 8–10 ins deep – that is, if you measure from the top of the ridges on either side. These ridges should be flat-topped, so that along them you will be able to grow catch crops like shallots, lettuces and French beans.

See that each plant is set carefully, with its ball of soil still attached. After planting firm the plant well, and then, having completed planting the trench, give it a thorough watering. If you get very hot, sunny weather over the next few days, cover the trench up with brown paper until the plants get established. You may have to water again three days later, and after this, unless it rains, a good flooding once a week will be advisable.

During the summer keep the rows free from weeds, and remove any side growths (suckers) coming from the base.

EARTHING UP

This is a special operation which consists of taking the soil from the ridges and bringing it up to the plants. The celery plant must be grasped firmly with one hand while the soil is put into position. You do not want soil to get in between the stems. For this reason it is usual to chop the earth up, and let it dry for an hour or two before it is worked into its new position. It is better to earth up in two or three operations – the first one when the plants are over 1 ft high. This may be in the middle of August. Another earthing may be done three weeks or so later, and the final earthing is usually completed in October. At this last earthing the whole of the stems are covered, the soil being brought right up to the top leaves. The ridges should now be smooth and steep, so that the rain is carried away quickly.

Just a few 'don'ts'. Don't allow any soil to get into the heart of the plant – if you are worried about this, get someone to grip the plant with both hands while you do the soiling up. At the first earthing do not soil up higher than, say, halfway up the stem. Never earth when the plants or the soil are wet.

There is no reason at all why celery should not stay in its trenches until the end of January or the middle of February following. To prevent early decay setting in, it is not a bad idea to cover the green tops with straw – firstly to prevent the rain getting down, and secondly to give a protection against hard frosts.

GREEN CELERY

To save all this trench digging and earthing up, you can grow American green celery which is planted on top of the soil when covered with powdery compost or sedge peat 1 in. deep. This celery needs to be planted in rows 1 ft apart allowing 1 ft apart in the rows. Plant about the middle of May and water it abundantly.

MANURING

Adding large quantities of compost to the bottom of the trench has already been mentioned. After this, manure water is perhaps the most convenient method of feeding. This may be either liquid Farmura or liquid seaweed. This should be put on from, say 15 July – four times at fortnightly intervals.

VARIETIES

Dwarf White: small, late, delicious.
Giant Prize Pink: large, crisp, sweet in flavour.
Giant Red: large, tall, solid, fine flavour.
Standard Bearer: large, firm head, good flavour.
Greensnap: does not require earthing up, meaty, crisp and stringless.
Golden Self Blanching: compact, crisp, nutty, does not need earthing up.

LEEKS

Leeks are always thought of as a speciality for Welshmen, but if you live in the northern counties of England you will know that there are a large number of leek societies which encourage the growing of giant leeks. They always grow best when they have plenty of moisture, but this must not be stagnant water. Well-drained land, then, is necessary, but there should be plenty of organic material present, not only as a plant food but also for its moisture-retaining properties.

SOIL

Leeks will grow on most soils provided they are deeply worked. They will not grow to perfection on very light sands, or on badly drained clays.

SEED SOWING

The seed is sown about the middle of March in the south, often outside, but north of the midlands usually in frames. If sown in the open, the drills are 18 ins apart, and if in frames, 9 ins apart. When the seedlings are fit to move, they are transplanted to 8 ins apart in such a way as to leave the remaining plants at that distance in the original bed. The seedlings are usually left in this bed until they are 6–9 ins high.

GENERAL CULTIVATION

The ground where the leeks are to be grown in the ordinary way should be well composted. After this, drills can be made 12 ins apart and 6 ins deep, and the leeks planted in these at 8-in. distances. Another method is to make holes with a dibber about 9 ins deep, at the above distances apart, the leeks being dropped into the bottom of the hole. The holes are not filled in, but the plants soon get a fresh hold and grow away.

If you want to produce large leeks, trenches should be dug out to a spade's width, in the same way as for celery. The trenches are 2 ft apart. Compost is forked into the bottom of the trench, and at the end of this operation the trench should be 6 ins deep. In this the leeks are planted 12 ins apart. As the plant grows, the trenches are filled in gradually in order to blanch the stem. Further earthing up is done right up to the base of the leaves as necessary.

Try to do the transplanting during a showery period, or water the trenches or drills well. Regular watering may be done in dry weather and liquid seaweed or Farmura can be given from time to time as a feed.

Keep the ground hoed all the time, and if the leaves tend to droop onto the soil they may be shortened back.

MANURING

Without a doubt the main requirement of leeks is to have plenty of organic manure in the form of compost. (I also give dry poultry manure at 1 oz to the square yard.) In addition to this, you can apply 3 oz of a good fish manure per square yard, when the leeks have been established for about two months. Give another dressing of liquid manure in addition in a month's time.

STORING

Leeks can be left in the ground right up to the end of February, but, if it is necessary to clear the ground for other crops, they can be stored for a month heeled in, in sand or soil.

VARIETIES

Regius: an early, suitable for the south only.
Marble Pillar: large, solid white stems.
Giant Musselburgh: a good all-round variety.
Lyon: stems long and thick, free from coarseness.

ONIONS

SOIL

Onions seem to prefer a sandy loam, but, whatever happens, they must have a very deep root run.

SEED SOWING

Seed can be sown at three different periods: (1) August, either to provide salad or spring onions early the following year or to produce fair-sized bulbs the following summer (different varieties are chosen for the two purposes); (2) March, out of doors; this sowing provides for the bulk of the ordinary bulbs that we use for cooking; (3) January, these are sown in boxes under glass and produce. giant onions, the seedlings being pricked out 2 ins square, when they are 1 in. or so high, into further boxes containing sandy compost. As with leeks, some growers prick them out into 3-in. pots, and plant them out from these.

When the seed is sown outside, take care that the surface is dry and friable. It is necessary to have firm soil. Be careful not to tread the soil down if the soil is in any way sticky. The seed is sown in rows about 12 ins apart, the plants being thinned out either 4 ins apart or 6 ins, according to the variety. The drills must be shallow.

In the case of spring onions, no thinning is done, the plants being pulled in the spring *en masse*. The autumn-sown varieties that you are hoping to use 'bulbed up' can be transplanted in the spring, say 15 ins between the rows, and 9 ins between the plants.

SETS

Instead of sowing seed you can buy sets, which are planted in a similar way to shallots, in rows 15 ins apart, with 6 ins in the rows. Unfortunately some of these go to seed but, if the flowering head is cut away as soon as it is seen, a fair-sized bulb results. This method is especially recommended for growers in the north of England. It is a way of ensuring onion fly control and usually you get well ripened bulbs as a result.

GENERAL CULTIVATION

When the seed is sown outside, as soon as the rows can be seen hoeing should start. If they are to be thinned, as in the case of the March sowings, this must be done when the plants are 2 ins high – first of all by means of a hoe, and finally by hand. It is usually after this thinning that the first attack of onion fly occurs. Never drive your hoe in deeply, and draw the soil away from the rows rather than up to them.

Those that are raised in moderate heat under glass (55 degrees F) are planted out in April, and if they are long and lanky some of the top can be cut off as well as a portion of the root. It is most important to keep the ground clean when growing any form of onion.

The author bending the onion tops to help ripen the bulbs

Depending on the district, it may be necessary to bend the tops of the onions towards the end of August, to help the bulbs to ripen off properly. Final ripening off is done by lifting the bulbs on to the surface of the ground, or laying them down on an ash path.

MANURING

A good rule to remember is that onions should have plenty of properly composted organic matter. This addition of compost should be given in the autumn. In March the bed can be lightly forked over, and, to add a certain amount of potash and to help provide a seed bed, wood ashes should be spread over the surface at the rate of, say, $\frac{1}{2}$ lb to the square yard, and raked in. Poultry manure is good if applied dry, at the rate of 3 oz per square yard, just before planting. Some people use soot or fish manure at about the same rate. Soot is usually put on with the wood ashes, but the organic fertilizers are put on ten days or so before planting or sowing.

STORING

The large onions that you want to keep throughout the winter are ripened on the ground, and then cleaned, have their tops removed and are stored in a dry, cool place. If you can rope them and hang them up under the eaves of a shed, or on the inside walls of some building, they will keep quite well.

VARIETIES

(1) *Autumn sowing*
(a) For Salad: White Lisbon or The Queen.
(b) For early bulbs: Express Yellow: globe-shaped.

(2) *Spring showing*
Bedfordshire Champion: a large globe, mild flavour.
Rynsburger Robusta: an excellent keeper.
Reliance: can be sown in autumn.

(3) *Sowing under glass*
Selected Ailsa Craig
The Premier
Crossling's Selected.

PICKLING ONIONS

These can be produced quite easily if the seed is sown in April, broadcast over some well-prepared land. There is no need to thin or to apply special manures – in fact, the soil should be rather poor. The crop is harvested when the onions are quite small.

VARIETIES
Barletta Barla: very delicious.

ASPARAGUS
Asparagus is comparatively easy to produce.

SOIL
It does best in a deep, rich loam, on the sandy side, but can be grown, of course, on most soils that have good drainage. On light soils, a little trouble will have to be taken in preparing the beds, and a good deal of moisture-holding material incorporated.

SEED SOWING
It is quite possible to raise your own asparagus plants by sowing seed. Dig the ground deeply in autumn, leaving it rough, and then get it down to a fine tilth in spring. The seed is sown early in April, when the surface is dry, in drills a foot apart, and 1½ ins deep. It is a good plan to put the seeds in separately, 3 ins apart. Asparagus seeds are very slow to germinate, and, to help you recognize the rows much earlier than you normally would, it is a good ideal to sow radish seeds in the rows at the same time. During summer, see that the seed bed is kept moist with watering, and the surface is loose by hoeing. At the end of the first year you should have nice young plants that can be put out into the permanent beds.

GENERAL CULTIVATION
The first thing you have to do is to prepare your asparagus bed. Add first of all one large barrowload of powdery organic compost to 10 sq. yds. Place this compost evenly all over the ground. If the soil is very heavy, and badly drained, see to the drainage first as you cannot grow asparagus in sodden soil.

A useful-size bed would be 5 ft wide, on which three rows are planted, 18 ins apart, the plants themselves being 18 ins apart also.

One-year-old plants should be put into these beds, early in April, 9 ins deep. It is usual to dig out a trench 6 ins or so wide, into which a special sedge peat compost can be put. Where the plants are to be placed a little raised mound is arranged about 4 ins high, which enables the roots of the asparagus to be spread out evenly and in the way they naturally grow. The trench is filled in after all the plants are put into position, and the rows are sprinkled with the fish manure.

During the season the beds will be kept free from weeds by hoeing or by covering them with compost or powdery sedge peat. During this time a sharp lookout should be kept for any plants that have failed to grow. If this is seen, the cause should be ascertained immediately. If the original plant is found to be dead, a new one must be planted right away. If this has to be done in the summer, soak the ground well afterwards.

As the foliage starts to turn yellow in the autumn it should be cut down and burnt.

When the beds have been established for two years, it is necessary in autumn to cover them with good compost to a depth of 2 ins. The loose litter from this is raked off again late the following February. As some soil may be removed from the beds during summer operations, it is customary to cover them with 1 in. or so of good soil when the excess litter is removed.

CUTTING

You will not get much to cut before the fourth year, and this is why so many people choose to plant three-year-olds. Cutting should start in April and continue till mid-June. Don't make the mistake of cutting everything that comes, as you must have some 'grass' to manufacture plant foods to keep things going. The method of cutting is important also, as care must be taken not to damage the crowns. Cut about 4 ins below the surface, and with a long knife. (A special asparagus knife is best.)

MANURING

Heavy dressings of properly prepared compost are required at the beginning and when the land is being prepared, apply fish manure at 3 oz to the square yard, and wood ashes at 8 oz to the square yard. In spring, when the plants start to grow, three applications of dried blood should be given at the rate of $\frac{1}{2}$ oz to the square yard, with a fortnight's interval between applications.

VARIETIES

There are both American and French varieties, but the following may be recommended.
Connover's Colossal: very large and early.
Limburgia: early.

Regence: large and vigorous, heavy cropping – a pedigree type.

SPINACH

SOIL

Spinach will grow on nearly all types of soil. The main requirements seem to be sufficient moisture, available nitrogen, and well-worked land. Under drought conditions it fails to grow, and goes to seed very quickly.

ANNUAL SPINACH

This is sometimes referred to as the round-seeded spinach, but it includes the prickly-seeded spinach as well.

SOWING SUMMER SPINACH

It is possible to sow this towards the beginning of March in a warm and sheltered position. Every fourteen to twenty days afterwards another batch should be sown to provide continuity. The drills should be 1 ft apart and 1 in. deep. As soon as the seedlings are large enough to be used, thin the plants to 6 ins apart. Thinnings are delicious when cooked.

If you soak the seed for a day before sowing, it will start into growth much more quickly.

SOWING WINTER SPINACH

This should be sown from the first of August to mid-September at periods of fourteen to twenty days. Prepare the soil well, and if you have heavy soil it is better to ridge up the beds where the seed is to be sown. The seed is sown in rows 9 ins apart, and is thinned like the summer spinach, but to only 4 ins apart.

GENERAL CULTIVATION

Hoe the rows regularly, or mulch these rows with brown powdery compost or sedge peat an inch deep.

Winter spinach usually has to be protected in the north and exposed parts, and this can be done either by covering with frames or cloches or by using straw or bracken. Beginners often make the mistake of picking the winter crop too hard. Care should be taken not to remove more than a moderate proportion of leaves from each plant.

MANURING

Add plenty of well-rotted compost, remembering that you

want ample root run and sufficient moisture-holding material. Spinach should grow quickly, and should be given liquid feeding if necessary. Watering with weak liquid manure is useful once a week in the summer.

VARIETIES

Summer
Monarch Long Standing: round-seeded, large leaves.
Reliance: very large leaves, long standing.

Winter
Broad Leaved Prickly: very large, dark green, thick leaves.

SPINACH BEET
Sometimes called perpetual spinach as it produces a continuous supply of large succulent leaves during hot summers.

MANURING
As for beetroot.

SEED SOWING
April–August. The rows should be 15 ins apart and the plants thinned to 8 ins apart.

GENERAL CULTIVATION
As for other spinach.

SEAKALE SPINACH
So called because the large white midribs of the leaves can be cooked separately and served as seakale, while the green part is cooked and served as spinach.

It is grown exactly as spinach beet, except that the plants should be thinned to 12 ins apart, and not be sown in the autumn.

NEW ZEALAND SPINACH
This will not stand any frost, so the seed has to be sown in boxes at the end of March, under glass. When the plants are large enough to handle, they are potted up into 3-in. pots, and, after being hardened off, are planted out in the open at the end of May. Readers with no greenhouse can either raise the plants in frames or sow the seed out of doors about the middle of May. Because the plants scramble over the surface

New Zealand spinach

of the ground, and are very strong growing, they need 3 ft between the rows and 3 ft between the plants.

GENERAL CULTIVATION
Little needs to be done, as the plants will soon cover the ground with a 'mat'. Picking must be done regularly. Instead of picking off the leaves in the ordinary way, the growing points are pinched back so that the part used is about 2 ins long. The result is that new stems are sent out. The growing points are very tender and delicious.

This is an excellent spinach for a dry summer as it does not go to seed.

RHUBARB

This must be considered a permanent crop, as it can easily remain in its bed for eight years, provided it is well manured. It grows well in town gardens.

SOIL

Choose, if possible, a deep soil, and add plenty of compost as a top dressing. Propagation is effected by splitting up the old stools, and 'crowns', as they are called, can be bought of various varieties. If you wish to increase the stock of rhubarb you already have, cut up the stools into four or five pieces, each portion having at least one good bud. This is best done in March.

GENERAL CULTIVATION

When the bed is ready, rhubarb planting crowns should be put in firmly, 3 ft between the rows and 2 ft 6 ins between the plants.

While it remains possible to get down between the rows, hoe them, unless the rows have been well mulched with sedge peat. In the winter, fork over the ground between the rows, and give each plant a good dressing of brown, powdery compost.

If flower stems appear, remove them immediately, as seeding only exhausts the plant.

PULLING

Never gather any stalks the first season after planting. Be sparing even in the second year. Be careful not to tear the crown when pulling: the best method is to turn the stalk slightly and then to pull downwards and outwards. Do not be tempted to go on picking rhubarb after the middle of August. You must give the plants a chance to establish themselves before winter.

To get earlier rhubarb than one would naturally, cover the bed or part of it with strawy manure. Clay rhubarb-forcing pots may be stood over the plants, with straw placed round about to provide the necessary heat. The rhubarb grows quite quickly inside the pots, and may be pulled when ready. Upturned boxes or barrels can be used instead.

MANURING

Regular waterings with liquid manure can be made throughout the summer. Every winter give compost at one good bucketful to the square yard, and in addition apply 4 oz of a good fish manure per square yard.

In the spring give 1 oz dried blood per square yard a week or two after growth has started.

VARIETIES

Timperley Early: the earliest rhubarb there is.
Hawke's Champagne: early, large and of fine quality.
Dawe's Challenge: good colour, forces well.
Glaskin's New Perpetual: one of the first to be pulled.
Prince Albert: early, long and thick.

MARROWS

Most people like to grow two or three marrow plants, especially as they do well planted on the rubbish heap. They do quite well on the flat in dry seasons, but in wet summers they are better grown on beds or ridges. North of, say, Manchester, they are often grown in frames, especially in smoky districts.

SEED SOWING

Seeds are usually sown in 3-in. pots filled with a compost of equal parts of chopped up loam and old manure. One seed is put into each pot, and, after watering, it can either be placed in a greenhouse, at a temperature of 50–55 degrees F, or be plunged in soil over a hot-bed. The plants are gradually hardened off until they are ready to put out in the open the third week in May. Seed may be sown out of doors under continuous cloches in April, where the plants are to grow.

GENERAL CULTIVATION

When planting in large quantities, set the young marrows in rows 4 ft apart, the plants being 3 ft apart in the rows. For this purpose the bush marrow is better than the trailing type. When trailers are used, they are often kept pinched back.

Keep up clean cultivation until the plants cover the ground. Mulching can be carried out with compost, spent hops or grass mowings about the beginning of June. Don't, however, put grass mowings on deeper than 1 in.

MANURING

Be sure to use plenty of properly prepared compost where the marrows are to grow. When grown on the flat, 3–4 oz of a good fish fertilizer may be raked in per square yard a fortnight before planting.

VARIETIES

Long Green Bush: striped, long, very prolific.

Rotherside Orange: flattened globe-shaped fruits, golden, delicate flavour.

Long White Bush: creamy-white fruits.

Custard White Bush: creamy-white, flattish fruits.

Early Gem F1: very early, heavy cropper.

Zucchini: early, heavy cropper, broad, long, emerald-green fruits.

Courgette: cut when 6–8 ins long and cook whole; heavy cropper if cut regularly.

14 Salads, tomatoes and unusual vegetables

TOMATOES

This vegetable is chiefly grown under glass, but in the south it is quite possible to grow tomatoes out of doors, and in hot, dry summers most people have heavy crops in the open.

SOIL

Tomatoes can be grown on both sands and clays. See that the drainage is perfect; add the right amount of compost as a top dressing. Do this in autumn, so that the soil is covered with the powdery organic matter.

SEED SOWING

Tomato plants always used to be raised in greenhouses, but the more modern method is to raise them under Access frames or cloches. In the greenhouse the seed is sown in boxes, placing each seed 1 in. square, but under cloches it is sown in the soil outside. When the seedlings come up they are transferred into small pots; take care not to hold them by the stem.

GENERAL CULTIVATION

It is usual to plant at the end of May, and the plants themselves should then be sturdy and hard and about 8 ins high, but if you are planting under cloches or Access frames, you can plant in April. Do not plant out without cover until the weather seems warm and settled; it is sometimes better to wait until the middle of June. Make a hole with a trowel sufficiently large to take the whole ball, and plant this so that it is about $\frac{1}{4}$ in. below the soil level. Soak the ground well afterwards.

As the plants grow, keep them to a single stem by removing the side growths which appear at the joints of the leaves, but be careful not to remove the flowers at the same time. You will need a stake or bamboo by each plant, tying it loosely to the plant with raffia. The plants should be 18 ins apart in the row, the rows being 2 ft 6 ins apart. The rows should run north and south.

Tomato growing in a whalehide pot

Dis-shooting tomato

In hot weather, mulch with your own home-made compost or sedge peat. It is a good plan to stop the plants – that is, to remove the growing point – during the second week of August, and as the bottom leaves turn yellow these too can be removed. Do not remove all the leaves from your tomato plants, though a few removed here and there will help to ripen the fruit.

During hot weather it may be necessary to give the rows a good soaking, say, once a week in the later afternoon. Pick all the fruit as it ripens, and if there is any fruit still hanging at the end of September gather it green on the trusses, hang it up, and it will ripen indoors.

Tomatoes do quite well when grown against south walls.

MANURING

Fork slightly when preparing the land and add bonemeal at 2 oz per square yard, plus fish manure at 3 oz to the square yard. In wet years a further dressing of wood ashes should be applied at 4 oz per square yard, late in June. After each truss of fruit is set, give a feed with a liquid complete tomato food like Marinure.

VARIETIES

Outdoor Girl: a heavy cropper, early, fruit of good size.
Histon Early: a good outside variety, very heavy cropping.
Yellow Perfection: a good yellow variety, excellent flavour.
Gardener's Delight: vigorous, heavy cropper, firm but with small fruits.
The Amateur: the best bush type of tomato.

CUCUMBERS

Cucumbers are usually grown in greenhouses, though they can be grown in frames and on ridges outside.

FRAMES

The frames should be on soil that is well drained, because they need heavy watering and there must be perfect drainage to take the excess water away.

SEED SOWING

Plants are raised in a heated greenhouse at a temperature of, say, 70 degrees F. It is possible to raise them also in a hot-bed, provided a bottom heat of 75 degrees F is obtained.

GENERAL CULTIVATION

The frames where the cucumbers are to be grown should be ready by the end of April. A hot-bed should have been made in the frame two weeks previously, by placing the well-made compost 1 ft deep in the soil. A 6-in. layer will be required, and this should be watered and trodden down firmly. A 6-in. layer of sifted soil is placed on top of this, and the frame and light are then put into position. A 1-ft square frame will accommodate one plant, which, of course, should be planted in the middle. Be very careful not to disturb the roots when planting, and, after watering well with tepid water, close the frame down for four days. Growth should start quite soon, and a little air may then be given.

Keep the soil and the plant moist by regular, gentle waterings, but never let the ground get sodden. As the plant grows, the original growths can be pinched back to get them to break. Four growths can then be trained, one into each corner of the frame, and, as they reach this, they should be stopped. Be sure to remove the male blooms as they appear, otherwise the female will get pollinated and the cucumbers will be bitter.

If the sun gets too hot, and the leaves scorch, cover the frame light with a straw mat during the daytime. In midsummer it will be necessary to syringe the plants well during the middle of the day, and again about teatime. After the second syringing the frame should be closed down.

Remove the cucumbers as they become ready, and, if the growths get too crowded, remove the older ones that have fruited, training the younger ones in their place.

Male

Female

Cucumber flowers

Training a cucumber up a fence

MANURES

Use the original dressing of compost, with the addition of a liquid manure like Maxicrop when watering, once or twice every week, when the plant is in full bearing. Dried blood is useful if a nitrogenous feed is required. This can be sprinkled lightly around the plants before watering.

VARIETIES

Victory: good shape, very dark green fruits 8 ins long, of excellent quality.
Butcher's Disease Resisting: strong constitution.
Rollisson's Telegraph: heavy cropping, dark green.

RIDGE

These are just as delicious as indoor and frame cucumbers if properly grown. Raise plants under glass in April to plant out at the end of May, or sow in pots and plunge in soil under cloches outside in April. Make a ridge by taking out a shallow trench, adding about 6 ins of fermenting manure, rotted compost, rotting leaves etc., and putting soil back on top to form a slight ridge. Ridges should be 3 ft apart and plants 2 ft

6 ins apart on the ridges. Stop the plant once when it has grown seven leaves. Hoe regularly; give a good soaking of water two or three times a week, according to the weather, and one feed a week with weak liquid manure. Mulch the ridges with straw, peat or lawn mowings.

HARVESTING

Ugly and distorted fruits should be removed at once, and others cut three times a week as they develop.

VARIETIES

Perfection and King of the Ridge: good types and heavy croppers.
Crystal Apple: round like an apple or lemon.
Burpee Hybrid: the best outdoor variety, excellent quality.

LETTUCE

People eat lettuce all the year round nowadays. It should be possible in an ordinary garden to keep up the supply over a long period, especially if there are cloches or Access frames.

SOIL

The soil should be rich in organic material so that moisture will be retained during the warm months. So it is a good thing to fork damp sedge peat into the top 2 ins of soil. All lettuces should be grown as individual plants.

There are two main types of lettuce – the cos and the cabbage.

SEED SOWING

Towards the end of August, seed should be sown thinly in a specially prepared seed bed, using only the varieties that will live through the winter. When these plants are fit to handle, they are planted out in rows 1 ft apart, and 10 ins apart in the rows.

If you have frames, the next sowing is made about the middle of October. When the plants are large enough, they are pricked out into other frames, 2 ins apart. These lettuces are then planted out, in the open, early in the new year.

The next sowing is made at the beginning of November, in frames, seeds being dropped in separately $\frac{1}{2}$ in. apart. Light soil is sifted over them, and the lights are put on the frames.

During fine weather the lights can be removed, though they should be put back again during wet periods. Water the soil well before you sow the seed, as you must not water once the plants are through. During frosts, shut the lights down, and cover with mats if necessary, but during warm periods air may be given.

For summer lettuces, seed may be sown in the open, either in the seed bed or where they are to grow, from the beginning of March onwards. Small sowings can be made at fortnightly intervals during March and April, or at three-weekly intervals from the middle of April onwards. The earlier sowings must be in a sheltered position in drills 8 ins apart, the seedlings being thinned out to 2 ins apart as soon as possible. Later on, sowings may be done in the open garden in rows 1 ft apart, the plants being thinned out to 10 ins apart. The thinnings can always be transplanted in other parts of the garden as and when necessary.

GENERAL CULTIVATION

Constant cultivation between lettuce rows is always necessary. Always handle lettuce plants carefully, as they are damaged very easily. When transplanting, never allow the roots to get dry and so don't leave them out of the ground longer than necessary. Take every opportunity of planting up odd bits of land and popping in lettuce plants between other crops if there is room. When transplanting, do not bury the plants; but do see that they are planted firmly. Larger-type cos lettuces often have to be tied round with raffia to make them heart properly. As a general rule, too, this type of lettuce needs far more watering than the cabbage lettuce.

MANURING

For lettuces that are planted out early in the new year, give 2 oz of fish manure, $\frac{1}{2}$ oz of steamed bone flour and 2 oz of wood ashes per square yard.

In addition to the liberal dressing of properly made compost that all lettuces appreciate, 3 oz of fish manure should be applied in the spring. As the plants get near to hearting, 1 oz of dried blood may be applied at 2 oz to the square yard, on the surface of the ground, and lightly hoed in. This is sometimes given as a liquid – Farmura being applied from the watering can after dilution.

VARIETIES

Cabbage lettuces

For sowing in October in cold frames or under continuous cloches:

Klock: tender, large solid heads.

For sowing in late summer for November cutting, or for sowing in the autumn to stand the winter out of doors:

Imperial: clear green leaves, solid heart.

Arctic King: good for the north, though small.

Varieties for sowing in the autumn to overwinter in the open and heart in the spring, but which will not do for late summer sowings and cutting in November:

Unrivalled Green Winter: dull clear leaves, inside golden yellow.

Varieties for sowing very early in the year for hearting early summer:

Hilde: fine heart, quick-maturing.

Varieties for sowing in the spring and summer only:

All the Year Round (badly named, for not a winter lettuce): firm heart, good flavour.

Webb's Wonderful: the biggest crisp or iceberg lettuce known. Should be more grown.

Continuity: a brownish lettuce of excellent quality, usually, however, not liked because of its colour.

Cos lettuces

Lobjoit's Green Cos: large, dark green, self-folding. A summer lettuce which will stand the winter under cloches or in frames.

Paris White: a winter lettuce sown in the autumn for hearting and cutting in the spring. Needs tying up in order to make it heart.

Semi-cos

Said to be a cross between a cabbage and a cos lettuce.

Winter Density: glossy dark green leaves, can be sown in autumn for cutting in spring, or sown in spring for cutting later.

Little Gem: an excellent type of semi-cos. Crisp, delicious, no waste.

RADISH

Radishes are often treated as a catch crop, as they are quick to mature. Aim at growing small, crisp, tender radishes, and not large ones that are full of pith.

SOIL

Radishes like a soil that is open and contains plenty of humus. They never grow well on land rich in nitrogen, so do not manure specially for them. On the other hand, they do badly on starved land.

SEED SOWING

It is possible to sow seed broadcast, or to sow them in rows 6 ins apart. Whatever you do, do not sow the seed deeply – 1 in. is quite deep enough. But after sowing do make the soil firm; you never get good firm radishes on loose soil. The first sowings are made during December in a sheltered, sunny place. Choose a 'short top' type. This seed is broadcast, and the bed is then covered with straw to a depth of 4 ins. When the seed has germinated, the straw should be raked off, and replaced when there is any sign of frost or snow. Finally the litter is removed altogether.

It is convenient to have these beds no wider than 4 ft, so that all the operations can be done without treading on the beds. The next sowing may be made in a frame on a hot-bed. Actually it is quite convenient to do this between other crops. For instance, if you have lettuces in a frame, you can take a crop of radishes from in between them without interfering with the growth of the lettuces at all. Do not make the mistake of thinking that radishes ought to be grown close together; they usually need to be 2 ins apart from one another.

Radishes always appreciate lots of damp sedge peat raked into the ground as it helps to hold moisture. Use it at a bucketful to the square yard forked into the top 2–3 ins only.

Sowings can be made outside in the open at any time during spring and summer. Sow thinly, sow shallowly, thin out early and do not let the bed get dry.

VARIETIES

Winter
China Rose: long, blunt-ended roots, exceptionally valuable.

Long
Icicle: a pure white radish.
Wood's frame: bright red, very firm.

Oval
French Breakfast: red with white tip.

Round
Turnip Mixed: bright colour, red and white mixed.
Inca: bulbs quickly, round, few leaves, very crisp.
Scarlet Globe: really scarlet, short tap-root.
Sparkler: the upper half of the root is bright scarlet, and the lower portion pure white, very dainty.
Cherry Belle: scarlet, globe shaped, slow to go pithy.

ENDIVE

Quite a useful salad plant, especially where winter salads are required.

SOIL
As for lettuce.

SEED SOWING
If you need endive in summer, you can sow out of doors at the beginning of April. If you are aiming for autumn and winter crops, sow at the beginning of June and July where the plants are to grow. The plants may be raised by sowing in a seed bed, rows 6 ins apart.

GENERAL CULTIVATION
When necessary the plants are put out into their permanent position in rows 15 ins apart, and 12 ins apart in the rows.

When the plants are full-grown, they should be blanched. Either tie the plants up individually, so as to blanch the heart, or lay a tile over the plant to blanch the centre. Plants may be taken up bodily, with a ball of soil attached to the roots, and planted in a dark shed. The ideal method is to place cloches which have been whitewashed over the plants when they are growing, and close the ends. This blanching takes three weeks or so.

VARIETIES
Green Curled: finely cut leaves, develops a good heart.
Green Batavian: broad leaves (lettuce-like), excellent.
Golda: very broad, erect leaves.

MUSTARD AND CRESS

This can either be sown in boxes under glass, in frames, or out of doors.

SOIL

The soil should be on the light side, and for boxes the compost usually consists of equal proportions of good soil and sedge peat. Add sufficient silver sand to make the compost porous. The soil should be made firm, and the seeds are then sown on the surface and mixed in with a wooden board. You can sow on damp sacking laid level on the soil mixture and stretched tightly.

Sow the cress three days before the mustard, as it is slower in germination. Be very careful when watering – the young seedlings damp off easily. It is better to soak the soil before sowing the seed.

Cut the mustard and cress when about $1\frac{1}{2}$ ins long. Do not pull it up by the roots, as it is very difficult to wash the soil off afterwards.

UNUSUAL VEGETABLES

If you are keen on vegetables, and want to grow variety, you will be quite interested in some of the more unusual vegetables. Here are some of the most interesting ones:

Asparagus pea: sow as for dwarf peas in the spring. The whole pod should be eaten when it is young and succulent.

Sugar pea (or mange-tout pea): sow as for dwarf peas in the spring. The peas are not shelled but eaten, pod and all.

Celeriac: a turnip-looking celery. Raise plants as for celery. Plant out 1 ft square. Give plenty of water. Not planted in trenches.

Cardoons: are grown like enormous celery plants in trenches. Raise under glass. Plant out as for celery. Blanch.

Sweet corn: eaten as cobs, seed sown in March under glass or under cloches, planted out early May, 1 ft square. Sunny position.

Potato onion: plant bulbs in well-manured land. Rows 18 ins apart. Plant 9 ins apart. Young bulbs are formed clustering around old ones.

Hamburg parsley: leaves are like ordinary parsley and the root like a white carrot. Sow seeds in March, drills 18 ins apart. Thin to 9 ins.

Soya beans: grow like French beans. Either cook bean pod whole when young, or thresh out beans when old and cook these.

Chinese cabbage: sow seed end of March. Use as greens. Chili

Celeraic – the turnip-rooted celery

is a good, light-leaved variety. Chee-Hoo is a dark-leaved variety.

Couve tronchuda (or seakale cabbage): useful for autumn. Grow as for cabbage. Plant out 2 ft square. Fleshy ribs may be used as seakale.

Salsify: sow outside at the beginning of April. Good variety Sandwich Island. A root crop. (For cultivation see salsify.)

Seakale spinach: has very broad leaves with thick white midribs. Sow April.

Note. Full details on these and other unusual vegetables are given in the *Basic Book of Vegetable Growing*.

15 Herbs

PARSLEY

Parsley will grow as well in light soils as it will in heavy clays. In both cases the soil needs deep working and manuring well. Light soils need firming.

SEED SOWING

For cutting in summer, sow in March; for cutting in winter, sow in June; for cutting in spring, sow in August.

Rake the soil down to a very fine tilth, and sow the seeds in rows 12 ins apart, 1 in. deep. Thin the plants to 6 ins apart. For winter sowings, rows need only be 10 ins apart, and the plants thinned to 3 ins apart. The seed usually takes six weeks to germinate. Germination will be aided if, when the soil is dry, the drills are well watered. As the plants take so long to come through, it is usual to sow radish seed in the drills at the same time. This enables hoeing to be done far earlier, as the rows can be seen.

A good tip for the winter crop is to remove all the large leaves during the middle of September; this enables large numbers of new leaves to grow for winter use.

In hard winters it may be necessary to cover the parsley with frames.

VARIETIES

Myatt's Garnishing: closely curled, dark green.
Bravour: dark green, closely packed leaves; useful for garnishing and cooking.
New Dark Green Winter: stands the winter well.

MINT

Mint will grow in practically any soil, and quite likes a north border. It is usually propagated by dividing the roots. These can be planted in spring or autumn in rows 12 ins apart. The beds should never be kept down for more than a year, as, if the plants are not active, rust develops very quickly. It is very easy to lift up the roots in winter, and to plant them in a greenhouse to force them on early. A few roots can be planted in pots or boxes and taken indoors for the same purpose.

Spearmint is usually grown, though Apple Mint is preferred by some people.

SAGE
This is usually propagated by soft wood cuttings made in May, or the plants can be layered in July.

Plant out 18 ins apart each way. Hoe regularly. Do not be tempted to raise sage from seed, as it will flower profusely and be less useful.

THYME
Thyme is propagated by dividing the roots early in April, or by taking cuttings at the beginning of September. It is possible to sow seed in April in drills 8 ins apart, the seedlings being thinned to that distance. Sow in a dry, warm position, or use as an edging to paths.

As soon as the flowers show, the plants should be cut, and the stems and leaves taken inside to dry. Sufficient growths should be left on the plants to keep them going.

TYPES
Lemon Thyme and Common Thyme.

16 Soft fruit

Though it may not always be possible to grow fruit mentioned in this chapter in a small garden, there is no reason why some of the soft fruits should not find room here. Some of them, like the redcurrant, can be grown as standards, and look quite attractive in shrub borders or as a background to flower borders.

BLACKCURRANTS
Now that it is possible to keep down big bud, blackcurrants will be grown more and more.

SOIL
Blackcurrants grow best on a stiff clay, but even this should be well drained. They do quite well on the lighter soils of Essex and Norfolk. The one danger is spring frosts.

PROPAGATION
It is very easy to propagate blackcurrants and all you have to do is to take. cuttings 9–12 ins long. These should consist of one-year-old wood, and cuts at an angle of 45 degrees should be made with a sharp knife to a bud at the top and at the bottom of the cutting.

Place the cutting in some light soil, burying it, say, 8 ins. Don't remove any of the buds, and be sure to take cuttings only from healthy bushes known to be heavy croppers. If you are going to strike a number of them, the rows should be 18 ins apart, and the cuttings 3 ins apart in the rows.

PLANTING
Plant at any time during the winter, using two-year-old bushes preferably. Make the rows 6 ft apart, and the bushes 4 ft apart in the rows. After planting, cut the bush down to the ground.

PRUNING
As the blackcurrant bears on the young wood, it is a good plan to aim at removing at least a fifth of the bush every year. In

this way it is kept growing vigorously and new wood is constantly provided. As the bush gets older, it may be necessary to cut away a third of the bush every year.

GENERAL MAINTENANCE

Put straw 1 ft deep all over the ground occupied by blackcurrants, or use sedge peat 1–2 ins deep. Keep a sharp lookout for big bud and spray with lime sulphur just before the blossoms open.

MANURING

Be sure to give plenty of powdery compost every year. Apply this in the spring as a top dressing. During the summer, dressings of dried poultry manure or fish manure may be given at 2 oz per bush in May and July.

VARIETIES

Mendip Cross: bears good bunches of fair-sized berries. The heaviest cropper in some areas. Makes a large bush. Early.

Daniel's September: a very late-ripening variety; the berries are large and firm. Grows well.

Wellington XXX: a cross between Baldwin and Boskoop. Long trusses, large, sweet berries. Vigorous, drooping.

Cotswold Cross: moderately large berries in compact, easily picked trusses. Crops heavily. Late season.

Jet: late-flowering, avoids spring frosts. Small to medium fruit on exceptionally long strings. Ripens late, hangs well. A promising new variety.

Mendip Cross: vigorous, slightly spreading bush carrying large berries on long trusses. Early in season. Crops heavily.

Tor Cross: higher yield than other earlies. Less inclined to fruit drop and berry splitting. Early in season. Cup-shaped and of medium vigour.

REDCURRANTS AND WHITECURRANTS

Because they bear on very short spurs on the old wood, they are both popular grown as cordons, U-shaped trees, and as standards. On standards fruit may be grown right the way up the main stem.

SOIL

They can grow on a much lighter soil than blackcurrants, and, in fact, seem to prefer light sandy soil to heavy clay.

PROPAGATION

Cuttings are made from wood taken from the bushes any time between October and February. They should be about 15 ins long, only one year old and well ripened. Cut to a bud top and bottom, as with blackcurrants. Remove all the buds from the base of the cutting, except three or four at the top. The cutting is then put into the nursery bed, which should consist of light soil, and planted 6 ins deep. Tread down firmly afterwards, and hoe out the footmarks. The reason the buds are removed is that you want to grow redcurrants on a leg.

PLANTING

Redcurrants may be planted 5 ft square, but in the case of Fay's Prolific 4 ft will do.

PRUNING

Redcurrants are pruned very much in the same way as bush apples. Aim at getting six or seven main branches; try to grow these so that the tree is goblet-shaped. Then spur back by all the side growths to 2 or 3 buds, the leaders being reduced by about half, and cut to an outward bud.

During the summer, just as the berries start to ripen, all the side growths should be broken off by half. It is better to break them than to cut them.

GENERAL MAINTENANCE

Spray as for apples in February. Keep the ground round the bushes clean by covering the soil with straw 1 ft deep or with sedge peat 1 in. deep.

MANURING

The principal requirements of these bushes is potash, so give wood ashes at 6 oz to the square yard. You never want rank growth in redcurrants. Every year apply a light dressing of compost, and give fish manure in the spring, at 3 oz per bush. Every four years give each bush 2 oz of steamed bone flour.

VARIETIES OF REDCURRANTS

Skinner's Early: the earliest redcurrant. Grows a long bunch of bright red berries.

Fay's Prolific: bears a smaller berry and a shorter bunch. The wood is very brittle. Early.

Laxton's Perfection: bears a long bunch of large currants.

The berries are pale, turning to a dull, dark red later.

Laxton's No. 1: bears a long bunch of large berries. The bush is robust, and the berries are bright red. A very useful late currant.

Wilson's Long Bunch. Large fruit. Well coloured. A very late currant.

Whitecurrants are treated in exactly the same way as redcurrants.

VARIETIES OF WHITECURRANTS

Transparent: bears large yellow berries on long bunches. An excellent exhibition variety. Good for walls.

Wentworth Levianthan: fine large fruit; very useful for the midlands and north.

White Versailles: bears large berries on short bunches. Very early.

GOOSEBERRIES

Gooseberries can be grown for cooking or for dessert. If you have not grown a really good dessert gooseberry, you should certainly try it, and the different varieties give a wonderful range of flavours.

SOIL

Gooseberries will grow on practically any soil, provided it is well manured and well drained.

PROPAGATION

As for redcurrants.

PLANTING

Plant as soon as possible after the leaves have dropped, 5–6 ft square. Spread the roots out evenly, remove the damaged portions with a knife, cover with soil and tread down firmly. Do not plant deeper than 6 ins.

PRUNING

In the first two or three years shorten the leading growths back by half, to form an open-centred bush. In the case of the spreading varieties, be careful to cut to an inward bud, and for the upright-growing varieties to an outward bud. Once the bush is formed, the only pruning that need be done is to cut

Inserting gooseberry cuttings

out sufficient wood to leave the bush open and easy to pick from.

For dessert varieties, when you wish to grow large berries, it is possible to spur prune – ie cut the laterals back to four or five buds every year.

GENERAL MAINTENANCE

Spray as for apples in February. Aim at clean cultivation. Do not dig round the bushes in the winter. Look out for caterpillar attack, and dust or spray with derris.

MANURING

Apply a good dressing of well-rotted compost every spring, and use 5 oz of meat and bone meal or fish manure and 5 oz of wood ash per bush each May.

VARIETIES

Reds

Lancashire Lad: fairly upright in growth, needs good soil. Oval, large.

Whinham's Industry: makes a spreading bush. Grows well under trees. A long, hairy berry.

Greens

Keepsake: one of the earliest berries to be picked. A good quality cooker. The berry is large, oval and hairy.

London: has produced the heaviest gooseberry known. Smooth skin; delicious.

Langley Gage: sweet and delicious when ripe. Greeny-yellow with transparent, large, smooth berries. Mid-season. (Not subject to American Gooseberry Mildew.)

Shiner: a mid-season variety. Makes a fair bush. The berry is very large, flat-sided and smooth. Excellent flavour.

Whites

Careless: grows a spreading bush. Should be heavily manured, as it is not a strong grower. Bears a large, oval, downy berry. Well flavoured. A second early.

Transparent: makes a fair bush. Probably the largest white grown. Smooth skin. Sweet and delicious.

White Lion Large: oval, excellent flavoured fruits. Mid season. Very strong grower which needs careful pruning.

Yellows

Leveller: the bush has a spreading habit. Rather a weak grower. Very sulphur-shy. Bears a large oval, smooth berry of good flavour. Mid-season.

Golden Drop: oval fruit of greeny yellow with slight 'down'. Flavour quite good. Nice, sturdy upright, but smaller than Cousen's Seedling. Mid-season.

New Giant: vigorous grower and a top dessert fruit. Has the Leveller flavour. Large, turns yellow.

Gunner: a medium grower. The berries are dark olive green striped with yellow. Hairy, Richly flavoured. Mid-season.

STRAWBERRIES

Most garden owners will want to grow a few strawberries. They need not take up a great deal of room.

SOIL

They will grow on most soils, though probably a medium heavy loam is best.

PROPAGATION

Runners are taken from one-year-old plants, once these have struck in the summer. The plants from which the runners are taken must be perfectly healthy. It does not matter how many runners are taken per plant as long as the parent is free from pests and diseases. In gardens, it is possible to sink 3-in. pots, filled with a light loamy compost, into the ground. The runner

Strawberry layering into a pot sunk in the ground

plant is then placed into this to root there. To assist rooting, peg the runner down with a piece of bent wire shaped like a hairpin. Once the young plants have rooted well, they may be removed and planted in their new quarters.

PLANTING

Never plant strawberries on anything but perfectly clean land, which should preferably have grown a well-manured crop previously. Plant in September, if possible, or at least in October, for unless you are on well-drained land in, say, the south-east, you will then have to delay planting until early next spring. The rows should be at least 30 ins apart, and the plants 18 ins apart in the rows.

Plant with a trowel, making a hole deep enough to take the full length of the roots; see that they are spread out and not turned up. After planting, see that the soil is quite firm, but never tread on the plant itself. Hoe out the footmarks, and keep hoeing throughout the year. If there is a severe frost soon after planting, the young plants tend to lift out of the ground. Take the first favourable opportunity to firm them in when the land is sufficiently dry.

GENERAL MAINTENANCE

Keep the land free from weeds. The first year, if you are not proposing to raise new plants, cut the runners off. In the autumn, powdery compost or sedge peat must be applied 1 in. deep all over the surface of the ground. Keep the compost up to the crown of the plant, as it tends to make new roots higher up the crown every year.

Next year, add more compost or sedge peat if necessary, and give a dressing of fish manure at 3 oz per yard run. As soon as the bloom begins to set, the powdery compost or sedge peat will prevent the fruit getting dirtied with soil. When all the fruit has been picked, pull up any annual weeds and thus clean the land for the winter. Keep mulching with sedge peat at 1 in. deep.

MANURING

Powdery compost should be applied every year in the autumn, and be spread evenly between the rows. In early spring give 4 oz of meat and bone meal per yard run, together with 4 oz of wood ashes.

VARIETIES

(Always buy virus-free plants of an Elite strain.)
Royal Sovereign: mid-season. Hardy. Fruit large and delicious.
Cambridge Favourite: outstanding in size, appearance and quality.
Cambridge Vigour: very juicy; medium size; excellent flavour.
Talisman: late, large, fine flavour. Strong grower; may give a second small crop in September.

RASPBERRIES

There are two main classes of raspberries – the summer-fruiting and the autumn-fruiting. Most people know about the former, but few seem to grow the other kind.

SOIL

Raspberries do best in a deeply worked loam. Wherever they are grown they must be regularly fed, and they do like moisture. They certainly like a cool climate, and morning mists and moisture seem to help swell the berries.

PROPAGATION

It is usual to propagate raspberries by means of the suckers that grow from their roots. These are sometimes known as spawn, and are really side canes. They often come up 1 ft or so from the original row, and can be severed from the parent plants in autumn and planted out. It is difficult to obtain raspberries free from mosaic, and, as this virus reduces the crop and the growth considerably, it is well worth buying material from a mosaic-free cane nursery.

PLANTING

It is very important to plant at the correct depth. Examine the roots, and you will soon see several large, spur-shaped buds, either above them or in them. These are the producers of next season's canes. Place these no deeper than $1\frac{1}{2}$ ins below the surface of the soil, and see that they are not damaged or broken off while planting. The rows should be 5 ft apart, and the canes 15–18 ins from the next. Immediately after planting cut the canes down to the ground. In the spring give a mulching of dung.

PRUNING

Newly planted canes should never be allowed to fruit the first year. Concentrate on producing really strong canes on which fruit will be borne the year after.

After this, as soon as the canes have fruited they should be removed and the new canes given every chance. In winter all the very weak canes must be cut down hard.

If the canes grow very tall, it is usual to cut them back just after the buds, which causes the canes to break lower down.

GENERAL CULTIVATION

In dry years it is very important to mulch the rows with dung or lawn mowings in May.

Every autumn, to keep them clean, apply compost along the rows, and in spring add some more compost or sedge peat and fish manure.

MANURING

Give well-rotted compost every year. In addition, give meat and bone meal or fish manure at the rate of, say, 8 oz per yard run, as well as 4 oz of wood ashes per yard run also. It is not necessary to put the manure exactly along the row, as the feeding roots spread out considerably.

VARIETIES

Lloyd George: not one of the best flavoured raspberries, but it's a very free cropper. An autumn fruiter as well as a summer cropper; the fruit is bright red and large. The New Zealand strain is virus-free.

Malling Promise: an early variety bearing large delicious fruits. A very strong grower.

Malling Exploit: outstanding, especially in the south-west. Long bright red berries, less watery than most types. Ripens early. Excellent dessert variety. Mid-season.

Malling Jewel: in the autumn garden the canes grow 8 ft high; a very heavy cropper, having a more delicious flavour than the other Mallings.

Malling Orion: a mid-season variety. A vigorous grower, bearing solid and firm fruit. Excellent for bottling and jam-making. Heaviest cropper of all.

Fallgold: the best yellow variety, which fruits for a long season both on old and young canes. Possesses fully the delicious, mild flavour of the yellow raspberry.

Zeva: fruits in July and goes on till autumn. The canes are self-supporting. Fruits large and richly flavoured.

Autumn-fruiting varieties. The only difference in the treatment of autumn-fruiting raspberries from their cousins, the summer-fruiting varieties, is that the pruning is done at a different time of the year. The fruit is borne on the canes produced in the same season, and so pruning has to be delayed until spring. The berries are gathered in September and October, and sometimes in November.

September: an American variety not widely known. Best available autumn-fruiting variety. Crops well with sweet, well-flavoured fruit late August until the frosts. Unsuitable for northern districts. Never fails to produce useful crops in dry soil and in dry seasons.

Hailshamberry: magnificent autumn fruiter. Canes bear heavy crops of strong growth. Season mid-September through to middle of November. Lovely dark crimson berries.

BLACKBERRIES

SOIL

The Parsley-Leaved blackberry seems to prefer a rich, deep soil, but the Himalayan Giant grows well on quite poor soils.

PROPAGATION

Select young canes the third week in August, and layer these

with the terminal buds still intact. The tips should be buried
4–5 ins deep, make a hole 6 ins deep and put in the bottom of
this a 1-in. thickness of leaf mould or fine soil. Then fill in the
hole and press down.

When layered in this way, the plants are ready for lifting
towards the end of November, but if not sufficiently rooted
should be left until early April. Sever the plant 6 ins above
ground level and on the side of the parent plant.

PLANTING

Make certain that the soil is free from perennial weeds. Plant
in a sheltered situation, and, if you are going to put in large
numbers of the Himalayan variety, have the rows 7 ft apart,
and the plants 16 ft apart in the rows. The cut-leaved variety
can be planted closer. Try to plant in November.

PRUNING

Every year the old canes that have finished fruiting should be
cut down to the ground, and the new canes are tied up in their
place.

GENERAL MAINTENANCE

Cultivate continually among the plants by hoeing. Flood the
soil from time to time in droughty summers.

Keep the young canes tied in position and out of the way,
to prevent their getting damaged.

MANURING

Every year, in autumn, add well-rotted compost liberally. In
February apply 4 oz of meat and bonemeal or fish manure
per square yard.

VARIETIES

Himalayan Giant: a very large blackberry, producing large
clusters of fine fruit; one plant is capable of bearing over 30 lb
of fruit per year. Can bear fruit on the old wood for several
years as well as the new.
Bedford Giant: earlier than the Himalayan Giant. The fruit
are large. Preferred by many as being better flavoured. Self-
fertile.
John Innes: the latest to ripen. A long picking season.
Ashton Cross: vigorous, with canes that are not particularly
thorny. Large fruit, attractive and deep black with the real

blackberry flavour. Late July–August.

Merton Thornless: no prickles on canes, medium growth. Excellent flavour, large fruit (often 1 in. in diameter). Mid-August–end September.

Parsley-Leaved: good variety for trellises and pergolas. Large, glossy, black fruit. Said nearest to the common English black-berry.

LOGANBERRIES

Loganberries can be treated in exactly the same way as black-berries. They are gross feeders, and will need heavy manuring every year. The loganberry is said to be a cross between the raspberry and blackberry. The fruit is firm and keeps a long time when gathered, and it is especially good for tarts and jam.